My Town's Feud

Adventures of a Misfit

Daniel J. Millette

Copyright © MMXXIV
Saskatchewan, Canada
Launch Publishing

My Town's Feud

Adventures of a Misfit

Editing by Shavonne Clarke
Cover art by Duy Phan

ISBN eBook: 978-1-7382324-2-0
ISBN Paperback: 978-1-7382324-1-3

danieljmillette.substack.com
www.youtube.com/@DanielJMillette
www.facebook.com/DanielJMillette

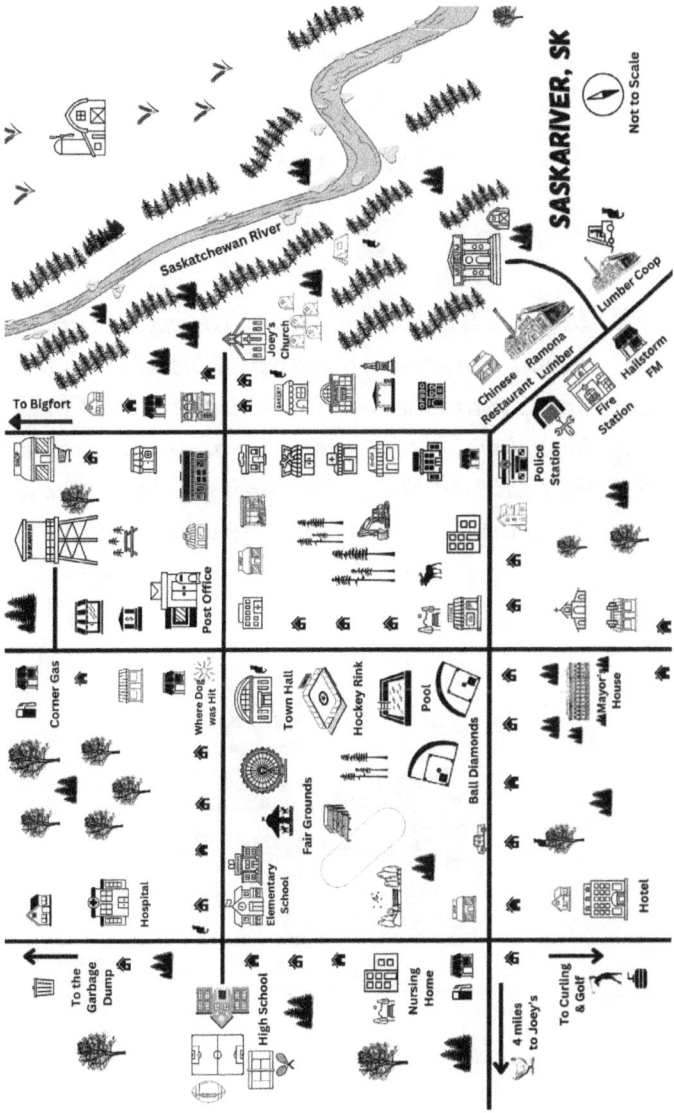

SASKARIVER, SK

Not to Scale

Saskatchewan River

To Bigfort

Joey's Church

Chinese Restaurant

Ramona Lumber

Lumber Coop

Fire Station

Hailstorm FM

Police Station

Post Office

Corner Gas

Where Dog was Hit

Town Hall

Hockey Rink

Pool

Fair Grounds

Ball Diamonds

Mayor's House

Hospital

Elementary School

To the Garbage Dump

High School

Nursing Home

Hotel

4 miles to Joey's

To Curling & Golf

DISCLAIMER

*T*his book is a work of fiction. Characters are fictional. Events are fictional. A bitter town feud involving Santa Claus firing bullets into a Christmas-themed water tower is fictional—or so we hope! IS THIS CLEAR? The author does not have time for petty fictional assertions claiming otherwise.

DEDICATION

To Joseph, the humble carpenter toiling away in
Nazareth.

Strength is found in silence.
Peace in perseverance.

A Thought

"...I was a young man. I hardly knew what I knew, let alone what I was going to know."

—— Wendell Berry, *Jayber Crow*

CHAPTER ONE

THE GAME

I, Joey Storthoaks, am the most hated person in my town. Hated more than old Mr. Johnson on Third Street. He trains his pet squirrel to attack kids if they breathe on his grass while walking by. Hated more than Christmas movie marathons...in July. Hated more than a government person, any government person. Even hated more than those two evil robbers in the *Home Alone* movies. They deserved the paint cans to the face.

But wait, there's more. I'm the most hated person in two towns. My hometown of Saskariver *and* our rival town of Bigfort can't stand me. And I'm only eleven!

Which is why I'm hiding right now in a lonely room buried in the innermost region of our hockey arena. Meanwhile, the hockey rink's stands are filled with Saskariver and Bigfort fans. They gathered for the hockey game of the century. One that would finally put an end to the greatest rivalry to exist since a man first married a woman. They don't care about the game anymore. They don't even care about fighting each other. They only care about hating one person. I hear faint shouts from where

I'm hiding. "Where's that Storthoaks kid?" "It's all his fault!" "Run him out of town!" "Kick his dog!"

I guess I united them for once.

I don't think I'm going anywhere soon. Definitely not out there. So, do you have a minute to listen to my story? One of a homeschooled misfit finding himself, getting too big for himself, and letting himself and others down. I can't guarantee a happy ending. We'll just have to wait and see. This is my story. My feud. My town's story. My town's feud.

※ X ※

"Do you have your equipment?"

"Yes."

"*All* of it?"

"Yes."

"You're sure?"

"Yes!"

"Let's go then."

"Uh, maybe I'll triple-check."

In my house, getting your hockey bag ready before a game is a lot of pressure. Once, my older brother Josh forgot a shin pad. Someone in the dressing room said they had an extra one he could use. Dad said no *thank you* and took Josh home. He missed the game. He's never forgotten a piece of equipment since. I mean, it only happened last week, but still. Lots of pressure.

As for me, I went to triple-check my hockey bag on this particular day. It was my big hockey game to play, and I wouldn't miss it for the world. I wouldn't even trade it away for a week of no school. Helmet? Check. Gloves? Check. Skates? Check. Cat? Check. Elbow pads? Check. Cup? Check. Good to go.

Cat?

Catman snuck in. Again. Catman is one of our twenty or more cats. Thirty or more? She's a sweetie, too—checking their gender before we name them is not our strength. We have cats everywhere at our acreage, four miles from Saskariver, Saskatchewan, Canada. Some of my favorites are Upside-Down Skunk, Little Mustache, Butch, and Catillac. I once named a cat after my sister, Ellie. Ellie died, and I buried her. Had a funeral right in the back garden. Ellie the cat. Dad said no more naming cats after siblings.

At my acreage, we have a dog named Doggy, a horse named Horse, and dozens of chickens with names like Brooster, KFC, HENry, and Finger-Lick'n-Good. We also have a baseball team worth of humans who live under one roof. Here's the starting lineup. There's my dad Marc and mom Geri (they're old, because all adults are old), followed by Johnny (17), Josh (14), Ellie (13), me (I'm Joey, age 11), Rebecca (6), Sam (4), and the baby Lyda. We're a big family near a small town where the prairie meets the northern forest. We love the outdoors, sports, adventure, getting into fights with each other, and being different. At least I like being different. Or, at least, I *am* different, whether I like it or not. But there's plenty of time to get into that. I must tell you about that championship hockey game I was about to play.

So, I chased that cat out of the way and hauled my hockey equipment bag—three times the size of me—upstairs. Dad says a boy will never be a man if he can't carry his own hockey equipment. My family was waiting. They were all coming, which doesn't happen very often. But you don't just stay home from such an event in our town. A championship game with the chance to beat Bigfort.

"Ellie, check that no chickens tag along," said Dad.

"And Josh, check that Sam tags along this time," added Mom.

"Joey, did you remember to close the door of the cathouse?" asked Dad.

I think I heard my dad say something at that moment. Maybe. I don't know. In my mind, I was scoring the game-winning goal, and the crowd was cheering wildly for me. Afterward, a National Hockey League scout walked onto the ice and begged me to join the Montreal Canadiens. He had a ten-million-dollar contract in his hand. All the while, Bigfort players were crying like the little babies they are, and...

"Joey? Are you listening?" said Dad.

What a strange way to start a conversation. I just nodded my head, and Dad seemed happy.

The Atom League championship game. The Saskariver Chickens vs. the Bigfort Millionaires. On a glorious day in April, with the sun still up after supper, and much of the snow melted away. What a day to be alive!

Officially it's Bigfort, Saskatchewan. But around here, we call them Big*fart*. Our forever rivals. We hate them. They're the worst. Worse than taxes, says Dad. Don't ask why I—*we* of the entire town—think that. They suck. They stink. Like a big f...

"Folks, here we are," announced Dad as we pulled into the rink's parking lot, as though we didn't know that already. "Go get dressed," he added to me, as though I didn't know that's what I needed to do.

I entered our dear old Saskariver Rink. What a charming place! You can look up on a clear winter night and see the stars as you skate. It's majestic. Character our rink has. A proper roof and a dependable ice-making machine it has not. I went to our team's dressing room to get changed. As I walked in, the old familiar smell of sweat, stink, and more stink hit me like a semi-truck.

"Joey's here!" shouted a dozen high-pitched voices around my age. "We're going to win now!"

I blushed and found a small nook in the room to get changed. The attention bothered me, as it always does. At the start of the hockey season, I was ignored when I entered the room. I liked that. But lately, something had come over me. I'd been scoring goals like a young Wayne Gretzky. Now, kids my age *wanted* to talk to me. Even though I'm homeschooled, and they're not. Dad says I must reply politely whenever someone says something to me. I'm working on it.

"Hurry up, Joey," said Coach Kevin. Usually, we have to call coaches by their last name, but his last name is Ziegelgansburger. You know, Coach Kevin will have to do.

"Hey, Joey!" called out Samson Hanson, our team captain. "Ryker says he's after you tonight. He said he'd hit you into next week. Said he's going to end your life. Said when he wins tonight, he's going to bring the championship trophy to your grave just to make fun of you."

I blushed. Ryker Hanson is the cousin of Samson. Ryker plays for Bigfort. He's an arrogant son of a gun. He acts like a surfer dude and even has long yellow hair. But in reality, Ryker Hanson's a hockey player. And as a hockey player, I hate to admit, he's very good. Better than I am? Maybe.

"Tonight's game plan is... we're going to play the trap system," began Coach Kevin. "We'll do the left-wing lock. Remember to neutralize the center ice zone. And dump and chase only when the defenders have coverage. All in the one-two-two setup. Ready?"

No one had a clue what Coach Kevin was saying. We're only eleven-year-olds. I don't think Coach Kevin even knew what he was referring to. Just stuff that professional coaches might say.

We walked out of the dressing rooms and onto the ice. Our team's pump-up music greeted us. The Chicken Dance. Our team is the Saskariver Chickens, after all. Our community baseball, bowling, golf, and football teams are also. We are all sponsored by the local Lumber Coop store. Coop. Chickens. Get it? It's better than the one year our team was sponsored by the Riversask Bakery. We were the Saskariver Riversasks then, with a loaf of bread floating on a river as our logo. Every time we won, Dad said we were real breadwinners.

The crowd exploded as we hit the ice. A red-headed girl my age, Evelyn Carnduff, started leading the Saskariver folks in the customary bird-flapping chicken dance. I noticed this. She noticed I noticed this. I noticed she noticed I noticed this... Where was I? Anyway, I took an extra-hard warmup slapshot. Not to impress her or anything. Nope.

Not at all. Evelyn who? I tripped as I swung my stick and fell over. The Bigfort people laughed. I blushed. She kept on with her dance. Not that I noticed.

What I mean to say is that the stands were packed. Well over eighteen hundred people were crammed in there, which is something for a town of about four thousand. Sadly, much of the crowd were Bigfort residents, which significantly lowered the average IQ.

"Hey, Storthoaks," called number one from across the ice during the warmup. "I'm like, gonna win, cha. Like, you can't beat me, man. Gnarly. Cha."

It was Ryker Hanson. Number one is usually a goal-tender's number. But as Ryker once told me, "I *am* number one, like, I may as well wear it, too. Cha." He added, "Like, my name is Ryker Hanson, but the girls call me Ryker Handsome."

I didn't reply to Ryker. This is the same kid who calls his birthday *Ryker Hanson Day*. His birthday is on December 25th. No, it's best not to get into a chirping war with him. He could out-talk anybody, especially a homeschooled kid like me. Besides, there was enough chatter amongst the parents at the game anyway. Threats. Accusations. Plans to destroy each other's gardens. Everything you'd expect from two rival small towns.

Before the game, the referee stopped by both team benches to give a short speech.

"Okay, Saskariver," began Referee Ron Spitballer, a local resident who worked at the Lumber Coop. "You sawed-off little runts better win this game on your own. I'm not going to help you! I'm a ref of integrity. And justice! I don't play favorites. Got that, brats? I just want *perfect* discipline. That's all." Ron's beady black eyes provided an intimidating impact. His short stature, not so much.

Ron also gave a warning to the Bigfort bench. The Bigfort coach cursed as Ron skated away.

"Mamma-mia!" came a gentle voice from the penalty box after the scandalizing curse.

Ron pointed to this penalty box, and the Bigfort coach blushed and shut his mouth. Our Saskariver priest, Father Wally Zsxyltchovskiwehveltskibetishly, was working the penalty box door for the game. I might've missed a few *Z*s there. A kind man of God. From Poland? Mexico? Something like that. There was no more cursing from the coach.

I took my spot at center ice. The puck dropped. The sound of skate blades cutting ice, sticks slapping hard rubber, and screams from parents, coaches, and the ref filled the arena's air. By the end of my first shift, Ryker and I had each scored a goal. It was going to be a barn burner.

I won't bore you with details. Needless to say, the game went on as expected. Tempers flared. Emotions ran high. A few fist-fights broke out. But enough about the parents. The game itself was a struggle. At one point, Ryker and I got penalties for bumping into each other. Father Wally asked me to repent of my violent outburst while I sat in the penalty box. He told me heaven was a place for peace and then quoted the Good Book. *"Love your enemies!"* Then gentle Father Wally gave me a blessing, and I promptly returned to the ice and scored. Whatever works! However, by the end of regulation, it was 12-12.

"Where's my left-wing lock and trap?" screamed Coach Kevin as we waited for overtime to begin.

"What does that mean?" asked Samson Hanson finally.

"It means play some *defense*!" screamed Coach.

For the first time, it hit us: if we played defense, we wouldn't need to score as many goals.

Overtime started. The goals stopped coming. Everyone wanted to avoid allowing the winning goal to go against them. So, nobody scored.

Second overtime. Still no change. 12-12.

By the third overtime, there was clearly a problem at hand. The game needed to end, and soon. You see, this was the last day of the season for the Saskariver rink. The ice was getting taken out the next day. Our poor ice-making machine can't run too long in the warmer weather. And we couldn't finish the game in Bigfort either. Their ice was already out, so they could host their annual dill pickle festival. Sour pickles sweeten Bigfort people up. But worse still, our Saskariver arena was booked at 8:30 p.m. for the figure skating windup party! We had to be out of there by 8:29 p.m., or the figure skating club would raise heck. They were powerful and feared by all. No, the game had to end by 8:29 p.m. It was added tension.

"Ref, drop the puck!" yelled a parent from Bigfort before the start of the third overtime.

"Quiet, Bigfarter!" snapped Referee Ron Spitballer.

"A blind zebra would be better than you!" replied another Bigfort parent.

"You're the blind one!" shouted a Saskariver parent. "Have you seen how your wife looks?"

Oh boy, things got nasty. The words were leading to shouts, screams, and pushes. A stuffed chicken got thrown on the ice. Followed by a Bigfort parent. Followed by an actual chicken. In the end, Ron Spitballer threw the crowd out of the game. That's right.

"Everyone out!" shouted Ron. "The game doesn't continue until everyone leaves!"

I looked on as nearly two thousand people spilled out into the night. Soon, all that remained was a single cat sitting in the stands. Catman had come, after all, to cheer us on! I guess I never shut that cathouse door. Why didn't Dad remind me?

"You too!" said Ron to the cat. Catman hung her head and drifted off to the exit.

The game continued. But not soon enough. At 8:29 p.m., Ron Spitballer blew his whistle fiercely.

"Everybody get the heck off the ice!" he shouted.

"Like, not fair, man!" said Ryker and his team.

"What do we do?" shouted Coach Kevin.

"It's a tie game!" said Ron. "You don't want to mess with the figure skating committee! We'll all be dead!"

There's an old saying: *A tie is like kissing your sister.* I believe it. It was the worst thing I'd ever seen. To tie Bigfort? In a championship game?

Dejected, we all went into the dressing room.

"Joey!" shouted a dozen teammates. "Why didn't you score another goal!"

I guess the twelve goals I'd already scored weren't enough. I sheepishly took my equipment off and left. Sad. Disappointed.

I opened the door to the parking lot and sidestepped a mini-riot. Parents were at each other's necks. Thankfully, my parents were hunkered down in the family vehicle. Catman purred away in Ellie's lap. We left. Such was my big game. A giant failure.

I blame Bigfort. I hate Bigfort. Like everyone in my town, I'd love nothing more than to see their destruction.

TIME

00:00

JOEY   RYKER

12-12

CHAPTER TWO

A CHALLENGE

"Joey!" said Mom as we sat together at the kitchen table. "Joey, focus! Where's your brain at?"

My brain wasn't in the kitchen. It was still on the ice at the Saskariver rink. It was the day after the hockey game, and I was still mad. We tied Bigfort. A tie! Like kissing your sister!

"Joey, you smell," said my little sister Rebecca.

Sisters. Hmmph.

"Joey, you *need* to write your persuasive essay," said Mom.

Moms. Hmmph.

I asked her why should I try to persuade others if she couldn't even persuade me to write the essay. Ha! She said she'd persuade my dad to chat with me later about that comment.

Dads. Hmmph.

No, my brain wasn't there. 12-12! Against Bigfort! I wasn't getting over it. I was never going to get over it. Not as long as I lived. Maybe even longer.

"Are you going to work, or what?" Mom persisted.

Yes, I was trying to put off my schoolwork. My home-schooling work. You see, me and my younger siblings do school at home. My older siblings go to school. Real school. Don't ask how. That's a story for another day.

"What are you going to convince people about?" she persisted.

"To blow up Bigfort!" I said.

"Yay!" shouted my younger brother Sam. At least he was on my side.

"Joey! Say something better. What's on your mind?"

I stared blankly for a while. Then I looked up at Mom. Her annoyed stare filled my vision. Hmmph. So, I said what was on my mind.

"Mom, I was just thinking..."

"What?"

"Well, you're not *fat*. Don't worry. But you're not *skinny* like you used to be either..."

There was...no explosion. Nothing. My mom took it calmly. As every child knows, *that* is a dangerous situation.

"Joey?"

"What?"

"I was just thinking," she began. "You used to be cute. But you're not anymore."

Pow!

"And since you're a bit hard to look at," she continued, "you will go outside to do your schoolwork. If you're not ready to write your essay, take your social studies work. Read the *Canadiana Magazine* for your next lesson."

I was *that* close to an easy exit. That close! I went to the living room to find the *Canadiana Magazine*. Stupid social studies. What did I have to learn about Canada?

I'd already read everything there was to know about this country. And I actually enjoyed that. But still! Stupid Bigfort. Why did they have to be part of Canada?

It was a warm day for April. The type of day that makes you want to stay out and drink in the sun greedily. Snow was melting. Birds singing. Eleven-year-olds grumbling. Stupid Bigfort!

I hopped on my bike and pulled out of our driveway. Doggy, our German shepherd, black lab, and collie mix, followed. I pedaled south a few miles. The gravel was firm enough that I could go forward without too much effort. Hmmph!

I decided to stop at the old abandoned Ukrainian church down our road. You know the kind? With the domed turrets that look like a head of garlic? Pulling into the yard, I took a look around. Not all the snow had melted from the cemetery, but at least the tombstones were now visible. There were rabbit, coyote, and deer tracks throughout the yard. Maybe even some human tracks. Some of the animal prints led right to the front door of the small white church.

I went up to the door and pulled the knob. Locked. That was just as well. I'd heard rumors of this place. One of our neighbor's kids, Jeff Tisdale—a hockey teammate—told me a story. I guess his family owns the property around the church, and he said he once went out in the evening and heard music coming from the church. Organ music. The thing is, there was no organ in this church. At least not anymore. And the other thing is, no one was around. It was a ghost.

"I don't believe in ghosts," I muttered aloud, trying to convince myself.

I plopped myself down on the ground alongside the exterior of the church and opened the *Canadiana Magazine*. After daydreaming for thirty minutes—take *that* Mom!—I started reading the open pages. What to see? An article on making maple sugar. Nope. A story about a lumberjack who built a custom toilet using only a pine tree and his axe. Too weird. A letter to the editor demanding that Canada invade the United States of America to take more of the Pacific coast of Alaska. Not the best idea. Not the worst, either.

I sighed as I flipped through the pages. What was I doing here? I wondered if Ryker Hanson was happy with the tie. Probably not. That guy is only happy with a mirror in front of his face.

Ah! I was distracted again. So, I quickly flipped through the magazine. An article finally caught my eye. It was an announcement and explanation of a contest. Can I recall it for you?

Canadiana-ville Contest Coming in Late Spring

Is your hometown the quintessential Canadiana-ville? Join the contest and prove it!

This spring, Canadiana Magazine is joining forces with Moose-Juice, where juice is a way of life, to discover what town screams Canada. The winning town will earn national bragging rights, two truckloads of Moose-Juice, and $250,000 in upgrades to community facilities such as hockey rinks, pools, and libraries.

The contest will be in eight stages. Starting April 30th, competing towns will submit pictures and reports showing how their town best represents Canadian symbols. One Canadian symbol will be judged each week; unsuccessful towns will be eliminated from the challenge weekly. At the end of seven weeks, there will be two communities remaining. A final mystery event will then occur. Our judges will personally inspect this last event and, from there, declare the winner.

The themes of each week are:

Week 1 - *The Beaver*

Week 2 - *Hockey*

Week 3 - *Canadian Flag*

Week 4 - *Royal Canadian Mounted Police*

Week 5 - *Diversity*

Week 6 - *Winter*

Week 7 - *Moose*

Week 8 - *Mystery Theme with In-Person Judging*

Does your community have what it takes? To enter, have your mayor submit an application letter. The contest begins soon!

I had Moose-Juice once. It was watermelon-rutabaga flavored. I spat it out. Disgusting stuff. I tried to give the rest of the bottle to my younger brother Sam, then to Doggy, the cats, chickens, anyone. Nobody wanted it. Horrible stuff.

"Horrible," I said out loud, closing my eyes and drifting into another daydream. In it, I was playing Bigfort in the championship game. Ryker Hanson was stickhandling a bottle of Moose-Juice, coming in on a breakaway. I snuck behind him, lifted his stick, and took the Moose-Juice away. Skating up ice, I fired a slapshot. The Moose-Juice went past the goalie, through the net, shattered the rink's plexiglass, and landed in the mouth of a moose. Then the referee came over, kicked all the players out of the game, and declared that both teams lost.

"Horrible," I muttered again, opening my eyes. Squinting into the sun, a light appeared in my mind. I had the answer I needed.

Jumping onto my bike, I raced home.

"Mom!" I shouted, coming inside the house.

"I just got Lyda to sleep, darn it!" she said.

Lyda started crying from the bedroom. I didn't care.

"Mom! I know what to do! I will write a purse-Asian, persagion, per-whatever letter to the mayor!"

"You're going to go get your sister and make her stop crying is what you're going to do," said Mom.

I ran to the bedroom, picked up Lyda, and ran back. She was wailing now. I had to shout to hear my own voice.

"I'm going to tell Mayor Nutrine to make us Canadiana-ville! We're going to be a moose! And a beaver! The flag and some other things!"

"Give me Lyda," said Mom. Lyda settled down right away.

"Do you think it will work?" I asked.

"Sure," said Mom.

I don't think she had any idea what I was saying. I got my pencil and paper out and started my essay. After half an hour, this is what I had:

Dear Mayor Karen Nutrine,

How are you? I'm fine. My name is Joey Storthoaks. I am eleven and i live on an ackeredge near Saskariver. I have three brothers three sisters a dog horse and lots of chickens and cats. Do you want to know there names? I scored twelve goals for Saskariver against Bigfart in the final game. So what I need to say is important.

Do you hate Bigfart? I do. There the werst! They make fun of us and there dum and i think there the werst! In fact all our poor children in town get hurt by Bigfart. For example they have one kid named Ryker Hanson who hits people in games even tho theres no hitting in our leegue! You must stop this ~~imedtiately immetdet~~ at once! Think of the children

We need to do something about them. Butwhat? I know!

We need to enter the Canadiana-ville contest! We need to enter it and win it and beat Bigfart so that we can show them were so much better then tham.

This is what we have to do? We need to spend weeks showing the juges that we represent there Canadaian symbols! We need to be like a beaver hockeytown winter Canada flag and moose and some other things.

Its really easy and the contest will bring us together to beat Bigfart and win. I have cut out the form for you to fill out and send in so that we can win. If you do this you will be a hero and Saskariver will finally be able to beat Bigfart and win.

Joey Storthoaks

P.S. Oh I forgot we also have to be like a RCMP police town or something. And a diversity town. That sounds easy

P.P.S. You will be famous if we win. So I think you should do this. Hint hint. I'll even get people to vote for you if you do this and we win. Hint hint!

I showed my mom the letter. After a ten-minute lecture about grammar and spelling, we fixed it together and dropped the letter at the town office. Two days later, I received a reply:

Dear Master Storthoaks,
Mayor Nutrine thanks you for your letter. She loves your idea of entering the contest and bringing glory to her work and to the town of Saskariver. The proposal will be motioned at the next town meeting.
Bob Yorkton,
Town Administrator

"Mom!" I shouted. "They might use my idea! Now you have to give me an A-plus on the assignment!"

"We'll see," she said. Sheesh! What does a guy have to do to get a good mark?

Three days later, another letter arrived. This one came from the head honcho herself.

Dear Master Storthoaks,
As the humble mayor of this town, I am delighted to inform you that, thanks to my hard work, your proposal has been accepted by the town council. We will begin preparations immediately. Thank you for growing our town and for helping me in the next election.
Humbly yours,
Karen Nutrine, Mayor

"A-plus, here we come!" I shouted.

I was about to file the letter when an added note on the bottom caught my eye.

P.S. The town council has decided to make you, Joey Storthoaks, head of the committee. You must attend all meetings, speak at events, and even help with the planning. Congratulations on this amazing honor!

I went blank after this. I hate crowds. I hate attention. I am a homeschooled boy of eleven. A drifter. A misfit, even. Nothing, NOTHING, in the world could terrify me more than...*this.*

Suddenly, Mom was right; I didn't feel so cute anymore.

Chapter Three

A Challenger

"Joey! Come with us! We're going to throw trees off a bridge."

I was at our hockey team's windup party. Good guys and all, those teammates, though I'd never hang out with them in real life. Just now, they wanted to throw trees off a swinging bridge. Because...why not? Right? When you have a bridge, you throw things off of it. Trees. Rocks. Cats. People. No, these teammates were troublemakers. And as everyone knows, I'm dead against trouble-making. Oh be quiet!

"Go play with your teammates," Dad said to me.

I left my seat at the picnic table and followed Samson Hanson and the rest. We jogged down a trail at our regional park toward a large swinging bridge hanging precariously over a deep gully. Some snow still lingered about the area, but otherwise, it was decent footing.

"Let's knock down all the trees!" said Jeff Tisdale. With that, a dozen eleven-year-olds started pulling down dead poplars and pine. Whenever a tree was taken down, they would march the tree toward the bridge and toss it over.

Crash!

Rotten trees explode when they strike ice at high velocity. If my mom was there, she'd say something like, "Oh! This is science! We're doing our *science*! We're learning about gravity!" Homeschooling moms love when everyday events can be counted as school. Like how weeding a garden becomes phys. ed. class. And it's biology, too. With some health thrown in there. Might as well weed the garden all day, according to Mom, for learning's sake.

Pow!

"Yay!"

Smash!

"Yay!"

This went on for several minutes. However, even destroying trees from a bridge gets boring after a while. Time to escalate things.

"Hey!" squeaked Jeff, hauling a sizeable poplar out of the bush while snot dripped from his red nose, "let's call this one Ryker Hanson!"

The team worked together at tossing Ryker over the bridge. Ryker splintered into a heap in the ice-filled gully below.

"More!"

Other Bigfort team members went over the edge, followed by their coach, the game's referee, the Bigfort mayor, and, finally, the caskets from the Bigfort cemetery. Soon, even this wasn't enough. Over the bridge went *our* town's mayor, Karen Nutrine, and members of the Saskariver figure skating club who had interrupted our overtime.

"Let's throw Joey over, now!" said Jeff Tisdale.

I shuddered. He *might* mean a tree and not me. *Might*. I started backing away.

"What's with you?" said Samson, turning to me as though a death threat was no big deal.

"I know what!" said Jeff Tisdale. "My dad told me."

"What's that?" asked Samson.

"Joey got us in some lame contest," said Jeff. "My dad just got put on the town council. Said Saskariver is entering a Canadian contest or something. We can brag over Bigfart if we win. Sounds like a homeschooler thing to do!"

Oh to be somewhere else. Like in a haunted church.

"Now that's something!" said Samson Hanson. He had a strange smile on his face.

Crash! exploded another tree.

"How's that, Ryker?" shouted Samson.

Yes, he had a strange smile on his face.

🍁 X 🍁

"Bigfart is in the *Canadiana Magazine* contest!" shouted Mayor Nutrine. "Who did this? Traitor! Murderer! Cat-kicker! Worse!"

"Mayor Nutrine," interrupted Bob Yorkton, the town administrator, "remember, we need to call them *Bigfort* at official meetings. It's not becoming."

An official meeting it was, with official representatives: the town councilors, Mayor Nutrine, and town administrator Bob Yorkton. Oh, and there was a timid little eleven-year-old boy named Joey Storthoaks. I wanted to be at home. But instead, I was in a collared shirt—thanks, Mom—listening to the town big shots talk.

"Someone there told them we were entering, eh!" It was Lorne Redvers speaking. In addition to being a town councilor, he also owned and operated the local radio station. "One of them there Hanson guys from Bigfart, er, Bigfort, found out. His cousin from Saskariver told him. I know this because it was reported to my radio station. Yes sir! At Hailstorm FM! The best and only radio station in Saskariver! Okaaaaay."

Samson Hanson. I knew it. He blabbed to Ryker. And to tell Ryker Hanson something was to tell the entire world.

"Let's sue them!" said councilor Blaine Neighbor. Around here, Blaine is known simply as Crazy Neighbor. His cowboy hat and beard gave him a rugged look as he spoke, though his eyes were kind and his smile readily given.

"We can't sue them," said Susan Humboldt, rolling her eyes. Mrs. Humboldt is the mother of Xander Humboldt, my brother Josh's friend. She's also a lawyer. Most people call her Sue.

"We need to do something! What if they win? What a disaster! We must stop them!" This came from councilor Dale Tisdale. Dale, Jeff's dad, was a big, strong guy, and he owned land, including the abandoned church, near our Storthoaks acreage. Dale hadn't lived there very long. He was originally from, I don't know, Humbleville or something.

If you're keeping score, there were five town councilors in total. Lorne Redvers, Crazy Neighbor, Sue Humboldt, Dale Tisdale, and...

"Yeah, oh yeah! Why don't we just win, or is everyone too lazy? Yeah." The fifth councilor. An honest man with an honest job. A Lumber Coop worker. A man with a clean-shaven face, a big heart, and an even bigger trumpet-sounding voice. Mustache. He might have another name—I hope he does—but in Saskariver his name is Mustache.

"Everyone!" shouted Mayor Nutrine, her red pantsuit outfit clashing with her even redder face. "I can't hear myself think. Be QUIET!"

The room, a meeting place at the town hall, was quiet. I sat there feeling sorry for myself. All I wanted was an A+ on a lousy essay assignment. I didn't belong here. I didn't want to belong here. All these adults seemed to do was argue and complain. I can't stand people who complain. It drives me nuts. It's the worst...

"Joey!" blasted Nutrine, waking me from my daydream. "Tell us again what we're doing here!"

I cleared my throat and spoke up.

"We're supposed to try and convince the contest organizers we're the top town in Canada. The most Canadian town. Er, Canadiana-ville. The place every Canadian would want to live. We must file a report at the end of each week's contest. And if we do a good job, we move on to the next round. That's it."

"But Bigfort is in the contest too now! Sooooo, what will we do there?" cried Lorne Redvers.

"I think we're supposed to beat them," I said timidly. "But being afraid of them works too, I guess."

Here I was. A five-foot-minus-one-inch boy with brown, messy hair and very little exposure to "the real world" trying to get adults to take some leadership.

"Lazy people here, yeah. Let's get planning. Yeah," spoke Mustache. Good ole Mustache. Lovable Mustache. The master of getting others to work.

"Fine!" said Mayor Nutrine. "What's first on the menu?"

"Well," I began, "the first Canadian symbol is..."

"I mean, what's our first menu item of *food*!" she interrupted. "You think I do these meetings without catering?"

Just then, a few people dressed in servers' outfits came waltzing in with carts and trays. There was caviar, oysters, lobster rolls, and champagne. Nothing that an eleven-year-old could stomach.

"Is there any food?" I asked.

"The escargot is to die for!" said Nutrine, shoving her face with another snail drowned in butter.

"Here, Joey," said Mustache. He pulled a chocolate bar from his pocket and threw it my way. "Yeah," he added.

"Yeah, thanks," I replied.

After fifteen minutes of frantic chomping and slurping, Mayor Nutrine continued the meeting. "So, what are we supposed to do?"

"Well, the beaver is the first Canadian symbol to showcase. We need to represent the beaver somehow within our town. Show it as a symbol and, uh..."

"I'll wear my fur hat!" shouted Mayor Nutrine. Her face was beaming. I couldn't imagine how many beavers needed to sacrifice their lives to make a hat large enough for her head.

"Fur day! It's settled then," said Bob Yorkton.

"What if animal rights activists find out?" said the lawyer, Sue Humboldt. "What if we get sued?"

"I think we're supposed to represent *characteristics* of the beaver," I spoke up again. I was shaking. I don't like attention. But I did like reading about Canadian history. So, I continued. "The beaver symbol goes way back. In the fur trade, beaver pelts were a common currency. Places like France just couldn't get enough of beaver hats. In 1937, the Canadian five-cent nickel had a beaver imprinted on one side. The actual beaver animal is a tough and hardy herbivorous mammal. It's the second-largest rodent in the world after the capybara. Beavers take down trees, build dams, and use their tails to slap warnings to others. Uh... They hold their breath for up to fifteen minutes." I was rambling off facts I'd learned from homeschooling.

"They have big teeth!" said Crazy Neighbor.

"I know," said Mayor Nutrine, "we'll have everyone in town go for a dentist's check-up the week of the contest. To honor the beaver!"

"And maybe we'll build a dam over by the Saskatchewan River," added Dale Tisdale. I think he was serious, too.

"We got lumber where I work," said Mustache. "We could build a beaver lodge or something. Kids could play in it. Or grownups. Yeah."

"And beavers are like submarines there!" said Lorne Redvers. "We'll buy a submarine. Maybe have rides for the kids. Okaaaaay?"

This meeting was going nowhere fast. I looked up at the clock. Another hour until my dad came to pick me up.

"And a diving competition!"

"Eat food that looks like wood!"

"And we'll rename our town! Beaverville! Yeah."

"Get a giant beaver mascot!"

"Who plays an instrument and sings falsetto!"

"The teenage girls will love that!"

Sigh. One more hour.

BIGFORT   SASKARIVER

Chapter Four

The Beaver

"Guys, we have to leave!"

My siblings seemed unconvinced by my pleading, so I decided to offer some motivation. I threw a shoe at them.

"Why? This is dumb," came their replies, as four shoes flew back at my head.

I was trying to get my siblings to attend the Saskariver Beaver Day. It was a tough sell. Probably, I shouldn't have mentioned the free dentist check-ups.

"We're all going," said Dad.

Ha! *The* final word. If they wanted to live. And off we went.

The festival was at Central Park, where the fairgrounds, pool, and other town facilities are located. My dad parked the vehicle. As we hopped out, three cats jumped out from the engine area. Our cats are like hippies: they like to hitch rides.

"$^@#! Guess I'm going back home," said Dad as he grabbed the cats and raced home.

The rest of us were left standing by the parking lot near the ball diamonds. We could hear noises and laughter coming from the main fairgrounds. Maybe this wasn't going to be so bad after all.

"Hi, Joey!" said Bob Yorkton. The town administrator seemed to be waiting for me as we walked by.

"Hi, Mr. Yorkton."

"Joey, the council has decided that you will be the official chronicler of the festivities! Here's a camera. Take as many pictures as you like. When you're done, you must write a report. Drop it off at the town office by Tuesday so we can send it to the *Canadiana Magazine* in time. Good luck!"

Maybe this day was going to be bad after all. Ugh.

"Take the camera, Joey," said Mom. "Your reports will be perfect for your school writing! English class!"

"Thanks," I said to Bob. I almost threw a shoe at him.

"Where are we going first?" asked my older brother Josh.

"Food!" said Ellie.

"We just ate," said Mom.

"Food it is!" said Johnny.

We followed our noses to a food stand with a long line-up. The workers were deep-frying a pastry. They called it beavertails. It was shaped like a beavertail, in case you were wondering. You could order whatever topping you wanted. Chocolate, sugar, cinnamon, marshmallow...all the food groups. When our turn in line came up, I couldn't contain myself.

"I want the Saskariver Sunrise!" I shouted to the worker. It looked amazing. Brown sugar, lemon juice, and a touch of cinnamon.

"Me too!" said a few of my siblings.

My mom smiled. "Perfect, we'll have *one* Saskariver Sunrise!"

"Mom!" we all cried.

"I'm not paying eight bucks for each of you," said Mom.

It's a fact that dads are most likely to purchase their kids treats for being such awesome kids. Moms? It's a fact they know their kids usually don't act so awesome.

Our order came, and we all got one bite of the treat. There should've been two, but little Sam sneezed on the beavertail, and one bite seemed fine.

I snapped some pictures, and we moved on. Sam stepped in some moose poo as we walked. Served him right. I laughed. He threw some moose poo at me. He laughed. Mom yelled. Nobody laughed.

"I guess Marty is here," she sighed. "Watch your step."

Marty is the town's celebrity. He mysteriously shows up at town events. Eats cake and smiles. Then, he goes back to the forest where he lives. Kids love him. As you can see, Marty leaves a big mark on our community. Several big marks. Usually poo-shaped. Marty is a moose.

We stepped around more moose poo—mostly—before arriving at the Saskariver Eileen Womanly Memorial Northeast Recplex Community Aquatic Recreation Facility at West Central Park. To save time, I'll just call it the pool.

At the pool was a giant water structure of sorts. How do I describe it? A big fiberglass transparent tank cut in half? Basically, it was a huge see-through boat. You'd hop on, and a pool worker would paddle you around the water. From it, you could see *into* the water.

The tank was so large that my family could ride together. We floated around for a few minutes. Looking down, the water wasn't the usual vibrant blue. It was slightly dirtier. Soon, I was able to see why.

Honest-to-goodness beavers were swimming around in the pool. I couldn't believe it! "Take that, Bigfort!" I cried while snapping pictures.

When we exited the boat, my dad was there to meet us. He was upset.

"I had to park way down the street!" he said. "They've blocked off the parking lot now. With a pile of vehicles trapped *inside* the lot. Who planned this thing!" He said this before remembering that *his* eleven-year-old son was on the planning committee. "Uh, I mean, what a great time! Golly!"

We doubled back to see the blockade my dad was talking about. It was a sight. A Lumber Coop forklift was racing about unloading lifts of lumber from supply trucks. The forklift was dumping the lumber into a massive pile that resembled a wall of wood. Like a...

"Beaver dam, yeah," said Mustache from the forklift as he saw us approach. "What do you think? Looks good, no? Yeah."

"Mustache," I called, "how are vehicles supposed to get out?"

"They're not!" he shouted back over the roar of the forklift, his voice sounding like a grizzly trumpet. "That's the point of a dam, yeah. It blocks the flow of water. It'll block the flow of traffic! I thought of this idea myself. Oh yeah! Didn't even ask the mayor."

I took a few pictures, and we left Mustache to his work. I felt uneasy about it.

Our next stop was the dentist's station. Ten dentist chairs were set up, and ten dentists were busy examining teeth. It didn't look like fun. I snapped pictures and pleaded with my mom to take us elsewhere first.

"Well," she said, "a dentist check is kind of like health class. But...I guess the lineup is too long right now."

As we prepared to move on, a man and woman approached. They were both carting wheelbarrows with boxes. They parked their gear near the dentist line, opened the boxes, and passed something out. I think it was candy. Sugar toffee? Strange.

We passed several stands on our way to the grandstand. There was beaver face-painting, a makeshift beaver hat store, beaver pelt displays, and even a beaver dress-up station. I snapped pictures of everything.

Eventually, we arrived at the grandstand. There was a horrible screeching noise coming from the stage. And I mean horrible! It sounded worse than that time Myrtle from church sang a solo hymn. If that's possible.

On the stage was a local band named Craven Arrest. They were actually pretty good. Especially the drummer. But they had a new singer join them for the day. The singer was short, wore a beaver costume, and sang like he was being tortured.

"This is soooo awesome!" screeched a few teenage girls nearby. "This Justin the Beaver singer is, like, soooo amaz-zzzzing!"

"I'm, like, seriously in love!"

"Like, seriously, right!"

"I loooove you, Justin the Beaver!"

Mr. Justin the Beaver was not, like, soooo amazzzzzing. He was, like, soooo annoying. He'd sing falsetto, quickly rap some lyrics, then hold a long high note with babyish emotion. Fitting. Every second word he said was "Baby!" It was a rollercoaster of horribleness, with death the preferred option. I even saw Marty the Moose gallop away from the scene. He was yelping a call of agony, which still sounded better than Justin the Beaver. I took some pictures and begged my mom to take us back to the dentist.

We walked back. Despite the earaches, this Saturday afternoon gave me enough material to write a solid report. Saskariver did well.

"Fire!"

All of us paused.

"Fire!"

We heard the screams again. They were coming from the entrance to the fairground.

"Let's go see," I said.

"Let's stay back," said Dad. "I have a bad feeling."

Dad led us to a nook in the trees with picnic tables. From there, we were out of the way. I stood up on a table and looked around. I could see everything unfold. What a sight it was.

Sure enough, Mustache's lumber dam was on fire. Flames from burning year-old spruce leaped high into the air. Through the screams and crackles, I could hear faint cries of, "Oh no! Yeah!"

People were gathering buckets, water bottles, or even boxes and racing to the pool to fill their containers. It was a desperate attempt to put the fire out.

The fire was bad enough, but it wasn't the only crisis to suddenly arise. At the pool, another problem was unfolding. The makeshift boat sprung a leak. People were sinking into the water. Lifeguards jumped in for the rescue. This startled the beavers who jumped out of the water and raced into the crowd. They weren't too happy, either.

The first thing the beavers did was spook poor Marty the Moose. Marty bolted away from the pool area. His escape route, however, was too close to the fire. A few sparks caught his fur.

"Marty's on fire!" I yelled.

Marty doubled back to the pool and jumped in. The splash sent waves out in all four directions. More screams ensued.

As if this wasn't enough, another crisis was developing. Yells and shouts could be heard from the grandstand. I looked over and saw the stage had collapsed. An army of teenage girls rushed towards the crumpled stage to save Justin the Beaver. The girls were all crying in fear and shouting, "like," "seriously," "like, oh," and so forth. Justin the Beaver was fine but indicated he needed help getting to his feet. The girls started fighting to see who could help Justin the Beaver first. The fight became a mini-riot. Soon, random residents were pushing and shoving with each other.

It was chaos in every direction.

"Who started this?"

"Bigfart will win now!"

"I'll hate beavers for the rest of my life!"

"I'll hate *you* for the rest of my life!"

The fire department showed up. As did the police department, ambulance services, and conservation officers. We had a real situation on our hands. It was beaver fever.

Oh man! What happened?

❦ .X. ❦

I was holding a cat in my arms. Looking out, I could see our chickens pecking away at our compost. One would grab an old piece of lettuce. Three other chickens would chase it around. Soon, there'd be a fight over this piece of lettuce. Never mind the large pile of compost still waiting to be pecked at. Chickens are so weird. Just like humans.

It was the following Monday morning. The Beaver Day was done. I was in shock. What had I got myself into? What had I got my town into? As much as I wanted to get back at Bigfort, this competition wasn't making me feel any happier. And now? I was supposed to write a report.

Little Sam came by to console me.

"You made *BIG* fight!" he said, holding his hands high over his head.

"Yes, I made big fight," I said. He wasn't cheering me up.

"We can fight Bigfart now!" he said, his eyes glowing behind his oversized glasses. "I'm getting tough!"

"You think so?" I said.

"I'm getting tough!" said Sam, kissing his bicep. "We beat Bigfart!"

With that, he turned and left. It wasn't much, but it was enough. Suddenly, I had motivation. Yes, everything on Saturday was a disaster, but it wasn't always like that.

There were some good moments. Enough to write about. And it's not like Saturday's calamity would repeat itself. No. There was still hope!

Dear Canadiana Magazine,

Joey Storthoaks age eleven reporting for Saskariver.

When I think of Saskariver i think of beavers. We put beaver dams in the middle of a road. We had beavertails to eat. We had beaver tours on the water. We had a beaver concert with Justin the Beaver. He wasn't very good. The girls liked him. Girls are weird. We even had dentist check-ups because we, like beavers, no teeth are importanter than cavities.

You see these pictures? They show that like beavers Saskariver likes to build create and have fun. Also like beavers sometimes things don't go as planned. There are predaters and bad weather and fires sometimes. To be honest we had a ruff day. A few things went wrong. There was fire pool troubles and some arguments. Some of the children even got cavities. Beavers ~~are resiilent reseleent~~ *come back when things get hard. Please give us another chance. We did a good job but will do even beter in the hockey contest.*

Gotta go! I need to go finish another delishus bottle of Moose-Juice!

Joey Storthoaks,

Saskariver, Saskatchewan.

"Mom!" I called out. "Can we drop this report off? Don't worry; I edited it pretty good already."

CHAPTER FIVE

HOCKEY DAY IN SASKARIVER

"Who started the fire!"

Mayor Nutrine was hyper with rage. She was also hyper with the dozen doughnuts she'd already demolished at the meeting. The doughnuts were her gesture to me. To show me I was welcome and all—because caviar isn't edible to an eleven-year-old. But then she went and ate almost all of them.

"We didn't start the fire," said Crazy Neighbor.

"It was always burning," said Lorne Redvers.

"Since the world's been turning," added Dale Tisdale.

"Yeah, I turned my head there, and it was up in a blaze!" said Mustache. "Holy smokes! I said. Yeah." His eyebrows were still singed from the event of five days prior.

"I hope you were fired!" said Nutrine.

Mustache started laughing at this comment.

"What!?" burst the mayor.

"Fired? Get it? Aww yeah," chuckled Mustache.

"Oh stop it. We're wasting our time here. Let's get down to business. There's only one explanation," said Mayor Nutrine.

"Okaaaaay! There sure is there," said Lorne Redvers. "What is it again?"

"Sabotage!" shouted Nutrine.

"What! Who?" said Crazy Neighbor. He seemed like a trusting sort of guy.

"Bigfort!" said Nutrine.

"Bigfort, of course!" said Sue Humboldt.

"I knew it all along!" said Dale Tisdale.

"Yeah, oh yeah," said Mustache.

"I'm ahead of myself, though," said the mayor, shoving another doughnut into her mouth. "Young Storthoaks boy, tell us where we're at."

I cleared my throat. Time to speak up.

"We sent the report and pictures in. There were over a hundred communities entered. But they knocked most of them out after the first round. The magazine could tell the fakers from the..."

"Hurry up!" said Nutrine. "Hair appointment at eight!"

"Um," I gulped. "The magazine sent me the update. There are ten places left. Three are in Saskatchewan! Including us!"

I paused as the councilors clapped, whistled, and cheered.

"So is Bigfort."

I paused as the councilors booed, hissed, and threw water bottles, cookies, and books at the walls.

I pulled out paper copies for all to see:

Saskariver, Saskatchewan
Bigfort, Saskatchewan

Humbleville, Saskatchewan
Hippiedale, British Columbia
Whalewatch, Newfoundland
Coolio, Ontario
Frenchisit, Quebec
Womanitoba, Manitoba
Curse Island, Nova Scotia
Notrudo, Alberta

"Is Humbleville good there?" asked Lorne Redvers.

"They're *very* good!" said Dale Tisdale quickly.

"What's next?" interrupted the mayor, not caring for the list.

"Well," I began, "the next Canadian symbol is hockey."

"Hockey!" shouted the councilors.

Before I could give a detailed explanation of hockey, with all its history and cultural development, Mustache had swiped the last doughnut from Mayor Nutrine's plate and was stickhandling it with his open hand. He wound up and took a slapshot across the table. Crazy Neighbor made the save and passed the doughnut puck over to Dale Tisdale. Tisdale went to take a shot, but Lorne Redvers deflected the attempt. The doughnut careened left, flying into Mayor Nutrine's open mouth.

"Mmblhkbhmm!" she mumbled, chewing frantically.

Sensing she was mad, Bob Yorkton butted in. "So, hockey? I guess we can do a community road hockey game. Maybe some face painting. You know, the usual."

"We could even bring in our local hockey celebrity!" said Sue Humboldt.

Gasps rose.

"You don't mean Jim?" said Crazy Neighbor.

"Sure do!" said Sue. "Jim-TheWin-Nipawin! He's living not too far away. Imagine! A Saskariver hockey player who made it to the semi-minor-pro league! And he won his team's most improved player award, back, to-back, to-back, *to-back*! What a winner!"

"Guys!" I blurted finally. "This isn't good enough! I mean, Bigfort has *three* local hockey celebrities. All played in the National Hockey League. Two of them won Stanley Cups. They also have a brand-new hockey rink to show-case everything. Saskariver, even with Jim-TheWin-Nipawin, can't compete."

"That's crazy!" said Crazy Neighbor. "What are you saying? Jim-TheWin-Nipawin's not good enough!"

"I'm saying we need to think outside the box a bit."

"Speaking of which, our doughnut box is empty," said Mayor Nutrine.

"What do you think we should do?" asked Sue Humboldt.

"I have an idea..." I said.

🍁 X 🍁

Going back to school was a bizarre feeling. Real school. My knees were wobbly with fear. Whose awful idea was this anyway? Oh wait, it was mine. I never thought my plan through fully. I'm only eleven. At what age can I stop using my youth as an excuse? Forty? Seventy?

My mom dropped me off at the front doors of the Saskariver Elementary School. She was excited for me.

Mom said walking back inside the public school was like a psychology and citizenship class all rolled into one. For me, it was simply the opposite of heaven. As I entered the familiar building, several students recognized me.

"Hey, isn't that Joey?"

"Joey Storthoaks?"

"I thought he was homeschooled?"

"He's coming back?" came one clear voice. It was Evelyn Carnduff. Red hair, kind eyes, and, for some reason, she was not one to look down on me. This always made me uneasy.

I tried to ignore all the students. If you ever want attention, act like you don't want attention. That is to say, I put my head down and blew right past them. I ran right into the wall next to the gymnasium door, fell back, and landed in a garbage can. They laughed. I shook off banana peels and pudding and snuck into the gymnasium, my face redder than Evelyn's hair. Not that I care about her. Got that?

The gym was packed—standing room only. Parents and community members were on chairs or standing at the back wall, while all the students were sitting up at the front, criss-cross-applesauce. I held up my camera and snapped a few pictures. This was my idea, for better or worse. Probably worse.

Within minutes, it was show-time. The lights dimmed. A spotlight shone on the stage. A familiar man approached the center, where a microphone rested on a stand.

"Okaaaaay, and welcome to this event here. My name is Stormin' Lorne Redvers from the local radio station Hailstorm FM. The best radio station in northeast Saskariver!

Okaaaaay. So, listen to my station. I play lots of good rock and roll and stuff. Elvis and Megadeath and other stuff there. And, uh.

"Hurray up!" came the mayor's voice from somewhere.

"Okaaaaay! Welcome to this here hockey day in Saskariver. We are a mad community. Er, hockey-mad. Soooooo, here we go. This is our first-ever school hockey draft. To explain, please join me in giving a welcome to large Mayor Nutrients, er, large welcome."

The mayor walked up and, of course, began with a self-focused political speech.

"Future of Saskariver! I am here for you! I care! My name is Karen, after all! *Caring?* No? Get smarter! Ahem. Although you can't legally vote for me yet, I always vote for you and your future!"

I snapped pictures—mostly of kids picking noses and pulling hair. Finally, the mayor got to business.

"Today is the first-ever school draft. Like the National Hockey League does every year with new prospects, we will do so in our school. Why? Because we looooove hockey so much. This event is sure to be a slam dunk! A perfect strike! A touchdown of homerun potential!"

I don't think Mayor Nutrine had a clue about hockey.

"We will begin with the grade six teachers. The three teachers will take turns selecting their students from the current grade five class for next year. Are you ready?"

The crowd cheered. A teacher walked up to the microphone.

"With the first overall selection in the grade six draft, room 602 is proud to select Evelyn Carnduff from Mrs. Simpson's 501!"

Evelyn Carnduff rose from her spot and went onto the stage. She was given a hockey jersey with a "602" logo. Then I took her picture as she posed with her next year's teacher, the principal, and Mayor Nutrine.

On and on went the draft. At one point, Mayor Nutrine interrupted the event.

"I'd like to announce the following trade. Mrs. Carter has traded Hudson Bayman and a fourth-round pick in next year's draft to Mrs Toeckes' class in exchange for Lucy Bobbyuk and a new dustpan and broom."

The morning wore on. It was exciting. The teachers sure loved it, that's a fact. By the end, they kept making trades, desperate to avoid having to pick the bottom few students. These last students didn't mind, however. We'd thought of this already. It was agreed that the last three students picked in each grade would get free slushies. Kids were practically begging to go last.

When the draft was completed, a celebrity appeared. Jim-TheWin-Nipawin hobbled onto the stage. At ninety-four years of age, he still looked great. What a legend! Saskariver hasn't had a successful hockey player since. Maybe I will be the town's next hockey star someday!

Jim-TheWin-Nipawin had a paper in one hand and his false teeth in another. He put the paper into his mouth, held his teeth over his eyes, and started trying to speak.

"Blmphsphh."

He took a minute, made the necessary switch, and continued.

"Hello, young hockey players. It's me, the back-to-back, to-back, *to-back*, most improved player award winner from my days with the Hastings Koolaiders. Or was that when

I was with the Meadow Lands Mallards? Anyway, young lads and lasses, just call me Jim-TheWin-Nipawin. I'd like to congratulate all of you on a fine draft day. Before I do, I have to read a bulletin handed to me by some strange-looking person before I came up on stage."

Mayor Nutrine's eyes bulged. This wasn't part of the script. What bulletin?

"It says here, uh," said Jim-TheWin-Nipawin, "oh yeah. Here. Greetings Saskariver. On behalf of the government, we must inform you that holding a school draft violates the Education Act. All participants may be charged if deemed necessary by the Ministry. Please vacate this assembly immediately."

The crowd gasped.

"So anyway," continued the speaker, oblivious to what he just read, "once when I was playing in the city of Worthington, or was that Windom? Walnut Grove...?"

"Everyone, go back to class!" shouted Mayor Nutrine. "We've been sabotaged! Bigfart, I hate you!"

"Bigfart, I hate you!" came the reply from the entire gymnasium.

Thus went my brilliant idea. A stick to the teeth is what it was.

Bigfart, I hate you!

CHAPTER SIX

HOCKEY DAY IN BIGFORT

The next day, I was on the road. Do I have to say where? Okay, fine. It was Bigfort. I was driving to Bigfort. Well, I was a passenger in the vehicle. With me was Mustache, Sue Humboldt, and Crazy Neighbor. Our mission from Mayor Nutrine was simple: to investigate. By that, I mean our mission was to sabotage. To sabotage Bigfort's hockey day.

I felt uncomfortable. I'm no saint, but I'm also not a dishonest person. I was taught to do things the right way, even if it meant losing a spot in the world if you know what I mean.

The drive was just under an hour. Mustache was at the wheel. I wish he'd have spent more time focusing on driving than talking.

"I spy with my little eye...something blue, yeah."

"The sky," I muttered.

"You read my mind, yeah."

"You're scary good," said Crazy Neighbor.

"Mustache," I interrupted, "why do we hate Bigfort so much?"

He slammed on the brakes. Our vehicle swerved into the other lane, then back, and finally skidded to a halt. Smoke from burned rubber wafted in the sky.

As our heart rates tried to return to a normal human level, Mustache turned his head to me and said firmly, "They hate us. Yeah. And we hate them."

I spy with my little eye something troublesome.

❧ ⚔ ❧

We arrived at the Bigfort rink, where a large crowd had gathered. Underway were the usual festivities of face-paintings, mascots, music, and cake. Nothing unique or exciting. It was precisely what Saskariver might've done—only better—if I hadn't spoken up first.

Bigfort has a new rink. Instead of a single side of yellow benches like Saskariver, red seats encircle their entire hockey surface. Like the NHL! Even better, the rink is connected to a pool with a winding blue waterslide, a massive hot tub, a children's splash pad, and a wave pool area. I'm not jealous. Not at all. I'm happy for them.

Those spoiled brats.

We parked our vehicle, and my travel companions pulled out a bag with supplies.

"Get at it, everyone! Yeah," said Mustache.

He pulled out a black marker and drew a dark mustache on his upper lip. Sue Humboldt put on a greasy hunting hat and camouflage vest. Crazy Neighbor removed his tattered cowboy hat and put on a fancy blue suit jacket and dark-gray toque. He even combed his beard straight and true. I didn't recognize any of them.

I rummaged in the bag and found a pair of dark-rimmed glasses. Why not? I put them on.

"Let's go," said Crazy Neighbor. "Aren't we a sight!"

We might've been a sight, but those glasses gave me *zero* sight. I bumped into two parked cars as I tried to make my way over. Once inside the rink, I tried to find a washroom to use. At first, I found myself inside a broom closet. Next, I stumbled into the women's washroom. At least, I think it was, judging by the screams. Finally, I made it to the correct location. I hope I did. Or was that a kitchen? Um, let's not talk about it...

It was now time to investigate, explore, and sabotage.

Crazy Neighbor was hanging out in the autograph section. Bigfort has not one but *three* local hockey celebrities! Wild Willy Michelle, Todd-the-Bod Fedchuk, and Ragin' Jayden Schmaltz. Crazy Neighbor was waiting to get his cowboy hat signed, which he had smuggled under his suit jacket.

Sue Humboldt went over to the raffle table. Items to be won were sticks, pucks, hockey tickets, and a stuffed toy baby that cried when touched. *Saskariver* was stitched onto the baby's clothing.

Mustache hit up the food concession stand immediately. He dove into half a dozen hotdogs.

"Gotta see what's so good about this place, yeah."

For my part, I went to the main attraction. It was a community-wide one-on-one street hockey challenge in the main rink—the ice being long gone. Two goalies were in place, and challengers played mini-hockey games on foot. The first person to get three goals would move to the next round. Ultimately, they were trying to crown the best player in Bigfort.

I entered and waited for my chance to play. When it came, I was matched against a boy two years older than me. He was strong, fast, and had a big mouth on him. I was short, quiet, and suffering from blurred vision. The game wasn't even close.

I beat him in one minute flat by a score of 3-0.

My next game came five minutes later. I was paired with a girl four years older than me this time. She was better than my last competitor; she scored one goal before I beat her 3-1.

My third game was a blur, literally and figuratively. I won 3-0, and the crowd really started taking notice. I could hear shouts and cheers. This was becoming a big deal. The fact that no one recognized me was the main cause of the stir.

"Who... Who dat guy?"

"Duh, maybe he alien?"

Or so I imagined the Bigfort residents talking like this. But one voice did stand out.

"He like, doesn't stand a chance against me, cha!"

That's right, for the final game, I was to play my nemesis, Ryker Hanson. Smooth-playing Ryker. I was in for it.

Goal!

Goal!

It was 2-0 for Ryker, all within a minute. What a blur.

I breathed deeply as the crowd roared to support the local boy. This wasn't working. As I saw it—or didn't see it, as the case was—there were two problems. The first was that my goalie couldn't stop a beach ball. He was deliberately throwing the game because he wanted Ryker to win. The second was that I couldn't see a blasted thing!

I did it, finally. I took off my glasses and got in position for the next faceoff.

"Hey!" a shout came from the crowd. "It's *that* kid!"

"The one from Saskariver!"

"They sent their best player to sabotage us!"

"Go Ryker!"

"Boo Saskariver!"

"You mean, Saskaloser!"

I gritted my teeth and dug deep. For me. For my family. For Saskariver.

At the next faceoff, I knocked the floor hockey ball out of the air before it even hit the ground, sending it through Ryker's feet, and I wheeled around him on an immediate breakaway. I did my trademark triple-deke, made the goalie lose his pants in the process, and buried my first goal.

"Hey, dude!" shouted Ryker. "Like, let me win."

"Not a chance," I said, winning clean another faceoff and barreling in for another triple-deke goal.

Tie game. The next goal wins.

By now, I was receiving death threats. Hamburgers were being thrown at me. One came right for my face. I reached up, snagged it out of the air, and took a bite of the greasy beef goodness in one smooth motion. Boy, did the crowd hate that. My only regret was that there was no ketchup on the burger.

The final faceoff came. This time, Ryker was ready for my usual trick. By that, I mean he cross-checked me in the throat, kicked the ball forward as I tumbled over in agony, and went in for an easy breakaway goal.

Not to be a floor mat to his success, I shook off my pain and twisted my body around. As Ryker went by, I, from my belly, hooked the ball away from him with my out-stretched stick. Ryker didn't even realize he didn't have the ball until halfway through a windup on a massive slapshot.

I shot to my feet, dragged the ball ahead, and came in for a breakaway. I dodged a bag of popcorn, a can of Moose-Juice, and that *Saskariver* crying doll thrown my way.

Approaching the goaltender, my instinct was to do an-other triple deke. But I knew the goalie would be waiting for this. So, I did something new, something I'd never at-tempted or practiced, something that probably had never been done in the history of hockey. I did a quadruple-deke.

Back. Forth. Back. And forth once more. This sent the goalie flying, probably to Kazakhstan, while I tucked the ball into the open net. I was the winner!

The boos and cries were deafening! Feeling inspired, I returned to the *Saskariver* crybaby doll, scooped it up, and held it over my head like the Stanley Cup.

I was about to need a police escort. But thankfully, shouts and screams could be heard from other places. This allowed me to escape unnoticed. I raced back to the vehi-cle, alive and mostly in one piece.

What this other commotion was, I soon found out. On the drive home, my companions gave me the details.

"All I did was ask where their gambling license was for their raffle table," said Sue Humboldt, ever the lawyer. "When they couldn't provide it, I suggested they might be in legal trouble. They started crying and throwing a hissy-fit!"

"And that was when I reached their celebrity hockey players for autographs," continued Crazy Neighbor. "Mustache had secretly dropped off hotdogs for the players earlier. Just set them right in front of them and left."

"Oh yeah?" said Mustache. "*That's* where I left those things!"

"So," said Crazy Neighbor, "I asked the players if their teams knew they were eating hotdogs. They blushed and got all upset. Eating junk food is a big no-no for NHLers. It was perfect blackmail. I didn't even know it at the time!"

"But people discovered we were from Saskariver when I started wiping ketchup off my lip. Yeah," said Mustache. "Wiped my mustache right off, yeah. They knew me instantly."

"That would've been the moment I beat Ryker Hanson!" I said. "So, they think we sabotaged them!"

"We *did* sabotage them," corrected Sue Humboldt. "Only we didn't know what we were doing."

"It pays not to know what you're doing. Yeah. Oh yeah."

🍁 X 🍁

I've been known to daydream while homeschooling. I've ended wars, solved world hunger, started wars, fought villains, and even found the Holy Grail, all while sitting at the kitchen table with an open workbook in front of me. My writing might be better if I worked on it more. *Might* be.

It was Monday after supper, and I was told to finish my day's schoolwork. Homework! I mean, all my schoolwork is homework, but still. Who wants to do more homework? So, after a sixty-minute daydreaming session, I immediately worked on my report.

Dear Canadiana Magazine,

Joey Storthoaks age eleven reporting again for Saskariver.

How are you? Im fine. Hockey. We all love it. We all dream of playing in the NHL. I want to play for the Montreal Canadiens when im older. But then I couldn't be my number nine because that's what Rocket Richard wore and his number is now retired and...

We had a hockey day in Saskariver. It wasnt at the rink. Are rink is to old for much. We need to fix it badly. Bigfort has everything perfect. We do'nt. I think we deserve it as much as they do. Or more.

I had an idea of having a school draft. I'm home-schooled so I didn't have to wrry about going to the wrong teacher. Unless Mom wants to trade me. Maybe. But the draft sounded like fun. Kids would get picked into different grades. They're were trades and everything. It was a hit! Even Jim-TheWin-Nipawin was there.

I probably shouldn't hide the truth. My big plan got ~~sabotoged sabatagd~~ *stopped. Some official said it wasnt allowed. I wish grownups didnt ruin everything.*

Sorry. Your probably a grown up reading this. I mean please give us another chance. As you can see in the pictures everyone had a great time.

I need to go to bed now. Maybe I'll have some Moose-Juice first!

Thanks for reading,
Joey Storthoaks,
Saskariver, Saskatchewan

CHAPTER SEVEN

THE FLAG

Saskariver made it to the next round! Unfortunately, so did Bigfort. I guess other places struggled more than us. I mean, Hippiedale, British Columbia said wooden hockey sticks destroyed trees and those evil rubber pucks were made from oil, so they had an environmental protest instead. And Curse Island, Nova Scotia, had some weird underground treasure hunt to find the Stanley Cup. They filmed it and everything. But the treasure hunt turned out to be a waste of time and money.

As per usual, our town council met to discuss the next round's symbol: the Canadian Flag. I'll just give you the "minutes" of the meeting.

- I told them the history of the flag. That the original one had a British Union Jack on it, and how the new one, with its two red bars and maple leaf in the center, was inaugurated on February 15, 1965.

- Crazy Neighbor got upset. He said he hated the Toronto Maple Leafs and didn't want anything to do with the maple leaf as a symbol. So, we agreed to have a "red" day instead. Mayor Nutrine was very happy about this. She reported she had some glossy red lipstick she was dying to try out.

- After Mustache suggested that the mayor would look like the devil if she wore bright-red lipstick, she threw her strawberry milkshake at him. She missed, but the milkshake smeared all over a wall. The red wall gave Crazy Neighbor an idea. He motioned that we paint the entire town red. This was agreed upon.

- Mustache was told to order red paint from the Lumber Coop. But Mayor Nutrine had him order a second load of red paint and sneakily "donate" it to Bigfort for them to use. She said their paint would be watered down first to make it turn pink in a day or two.

- Finally, Mustache said he saw a bullfight in a movie the day before, and it was very inspiring. He convinced everyone that Saskariver needed a bullfight. Red. Bulls. Get it? This motion passed.

As you can see, I just let them do all the planning this week. At least the meeting's food was good.

🍁 X 🍁

The clouds threatened to bring more rain this Saturday afternoon in early May. Nevertheless, the town was ready. Amazingly, the town workers of Saskariver got all the paint up where it needed to be. The town looked...red. Very red. Almost like it was on fire. Almost like it was h..."

"Hello!" I called to Mustache as my family walked up to the fairground.

"Oh, yeah, hello," he said, smiling warmly. His face was bright red, and his clothing was a devil's costume, complete with a red cape, red horns, and a red pitchfork. "This is the only red I had," he explained as my little brother Sam tried hiding behind Mom. "Wore it for Halloween back in high school. It's a little tight. Yeah."

"Oh really?" I said, trying not to point out the giant rip down his backside.

"Feel like the devil too, yeah," Mustache explained. "Nutrine made me drop the special red paint off in Bigfort at two in the morning! Yeah, it was so dark while I unloaded the darn paint. I dropped a can of it on someone's car as I tossed it off the truck. I hope the car was red already. Yeah."

"You probably just gave them a head start on their painting," I said, trying to console him. I then changed the subject slightly. "Whose idea was it to paint Marty the Moose?"

"Mine!" he said proudly.

"And who painted Mayor Nutrine's car?" I added.

"Oh it just happened, yeah. Some of the boys were painting Marty when he spooked a bit. Some of his paint dripped onto her car. Might as well paint the rest of the car, I says. Yeah."

My family headed to the grandstand and settled in for the afternoon activities. I think the entire town of Saskariver was there. A real bullfight! In Saskariver! The bull was pacing inside a cattle trailer, attached to a Lumber Coop truck, parked near the grandstand's horse track. Snoozy, one of the Lumber Coop employees, was stationed by the trailer, waiting for the secret spinning gesture to release the beast.

A worker opened the main gate to the bull ring, and Mayor Nutrine drove in with her red car, parked it in front of the grandstand, and stepped out towards a microphone. Seeing as the weather was cooler, she wasn't wearing red like everyone else. Instead, she was wearing a dark ankle-length jacket composed of leather and fur and a matching hat for her head. But her lips—oh, her lips—were redder than a cherry dyed in blood.

"Saskariver! You are the top town in Canada! Under my leadership, we are unstoppable! And that ain't no bull!"

Unfunny people should never try to make jokes.

"As young Joey continues to take pictures," she continued, "we will begin our first-ever bullfight!"

"*Ole!*" cried the crowd. Everyone had probably watched the same bullfighting movie as Mustache and knew what to say.

"And now to call out our matador! This fearless fighter of..."

Crack! Pow! went a one-two punch of lightning and thunder.

Rain suddenly fell from the sky in buckets. Not even a drizzle of a warning. It fell with a ferocity that only a prairie sky can provide. Soaking and saturating Saskariver and all therein.

Everyone in the crowd ducked their heads under jackets and hunkered down. It was an untimely storm. One which I will never forget for its abrupt start, its more sudden departure, and then for the aftermath it left behind.

Almost as if on a timer, the rain stopped after five minutes. The sun was already spilling out onto the crowd when I looked up. What I saw was a sight.

This town of patriotic red to honor the Canadian flag was no longer. In its stead was a princess palace of pink. The Pink Panther of places. A Himalayan salt hamlet. And not just a dull pink, but a vibrant pink. One might call it a hot-pink town.

"Oh no! Yeah."

Though everything was pink, Mayor Nutrine saw red. No microphone was needed to hear what she shouted. Turning to Mustache, who was standing near the track, in plain sight of everyone—it's hard to miss a big man dressed as a devil—she unleashed.

"You big dumb oaf! You took the wrong shipment of paint to Bigfart, didn't you!"

"Wait, no! It was dark, yeah."

"It clashes with my lipstick! This pink stinks!"

The mayor was boiling over with rage. With fists swinging wildly, she chased after Mustache. Everyone saw it. And Mustache, that red devil, ran like...heck. He was running for his life while Mayor Nutrine, wearing her massive dark fur, chased him. She charged one way, and Mustache bounced the other way. She spun around and charged at him again. Mustache took his cape and swung it away to avoid her fury.

"*Ole! Oooooole!*" went the crowd.

Another turn by Nutrine and a charge forward. Another duck by Matador Mustache.

"*Ole! Oooooole!*"

The mayor was tiring out, but her rage wouldn't let up. Poor Mustache kept bobbing and turning. Each charging attempt of the bullish Nutrine nearly ended his life.

When both seemed they could go no longer, the mayor took one final desperate lunge before crashing to the muddy earth in a heap.

Mustache looked down at the mayor. He looked up at the crowd.

"*Ole! Oooooole!*"

He held up his pitchfork high. To strike or to save?

A few thumbs went up. A few thousand thumbs went down. Mustache had been given the mandate. I sensed an election coming soon.

"Yeah! Oh Yeah!" trumpeted Mustache as he spun his pitchfork around, making the moment dramatic.

Sometimes, the stars seem to align for perfect chaos. Snoozy over by the trailer saw the spin of the pitchfork as the secret code, and he promptly unlatched the gate of the trailer. Immediately, a fifteen-hundred-pound piece of beefy anger plowed through the area's fence and onto the scene.

"Mustache!" I shouted. "Look out! Hit the deck!"

"But I'm in red!" he screamed.

"Bulls are partially color blind!" I cried. "The movies lied to you. Just don't move!"

This time, it was Mustache's turn to crumple on the ground. As he did, Mayor Nutrine saw him fall to the ground in a tiny demon ball and took the opportunity. She rose to her feet, scooped up Mustache's pitchfork, and started waving it wildly.

"*Ole! Oooooole!*"

Was she going to attack Mustache? Was she going to get attacked before she did the attacking?

It was the latter. The bull noted Nutrine's wild waves and charged after her at a hundred miles an hour.

"Holy cow!" she shouted.

"Bull," whispered Mustache beside her. "Yeah."

Nutrine dropped the pitchfork and took off in a flutter. The hunter was now the hunted. The bull charged once, and Mayor Nutrine swung her massive hips out of the way.

"*Ole! Oooooole!*"

The bull turned around to charge again. This time, Nutrine was already on the move. She sped to her car. She gave a quick pause before she arrived. Just enough to let the angry bull pass by.

"*Ole! Oooooole!*"

Jumping into her car, she fired up the engine and peeled away. She didn't make it far, however. The bull was chasing her as she drove. Left, right, stop and start. A dodge here, a hit there. A whoosh of air from a miss. A smash from bull-flesh smacking fiberglass. Just like that, a new sport was invented.

But the sport couldn't last forever. Something had to give. Above the roar, with my camera in my hands, snapping pictures at every moment, I called to Mustache, who was now cowered out of the way.

"Get the pitchfork! Smack that cow in the chops!"

"Hit the mayor?"

"No! I mean the bull!"

"What the devil! You're crazy, yeah!" he called. But he did what he was told. Scooping up the pitchfork, Mustache waited for his moment to pounce. The bull was still after Nutrine—or what was left of her car—so Mustache pranced over to the beast and gave the bull a tremendous whack on the nose.

The bull squealed and took off in pain. It charged through the fence once more, past the crowds, down the pink road, and was never seen again. And that ain't no bull.

When the pink dust settled, Mayor Nutrine sat in front of the entire town in her beaten-up car, her dignity and pride in shambles. It was another disastrous town event. Another sabotage from Bigfort.

"Guess this was a rare mis-steak, yeah," said Mustache.

Nutrine's shoe went sailing right at Mustache's head. Then she buried her head in the steering wheel and sobbed.

🍁 X 🍁

Dear Canadiana Magazine,

Joey Storthoaks age eleven reporting for Saskariver.

How are you I'm fine. Canadas new flag came in 1965. Red all over the flag. Red all over Saskariver. To show how Canadiana we are we had a red day. We also had a bull-fight because bulls hate red. I mean. Well, they actually don't even see red. And we love red. And. I'm confused.

It was a good day until it rained and then are red turned pink. And the bull got out and smashed the mayors car. I think it was Bigfort that did it. Do you?

My pictures of our day are interesting. I'm not supposed to brag but I think there very good. People stayed to celebrate even though it was raining. Can you give us extra credit for that? Please.

Well gotta go!

Joey Storthoaks

Saskariver, Saskatchewan

P.S. Is $20 a day to much to spend on Moose-Juice? Haha.

I looked at my letter after the last smudge of ink had dried. Red ink, no less. A nice touch. It was worth a shot.

If nothing else, I thought, at least my grammar and spelling were spot on.

Chapter Eight

The Ghost

"Honey, we have a crisis!"

It was my dad speaking. Shouting rather. I knew instantly it was a tragedy. He rarely referred to Mom as *honey*. Dad was away at work, and Mom was talking to him on the phone. We could still hear his voice loud and clear.

"What's wrong, Marc?" said my mom in a panic. She put her hand over her chest and prepared for the worst. "Who died?"

"Worse!" screamed Dad.

"Well, what?" asked Mom. "War? Pestilence? Your parents are coming to visit for a month?"

"Hey!" he replied. "This is no time to get into *that*. Your parents always stay longer anyway and at least *my* parents can cook, and... I mean. What? Look, it has to do with supper. Remember I said we were going to have company from out of town? Some guy from work and his family are in town for the day. I just found something out..."

"What!?" my siblings and I shouted.

Mom scowled at us. "Don't you kids have something better to do besides listen in? Scram!"

Things were tense. My parents hadn't been this upset since that one Christmas my brother Josh spilled the cabbage rolls all over the kitchen table, knocking over every piece of food, drink, and decoration with a chain reaction. Two of our cats, Doggy, and my brother Sam jumped on the table and started eating. No, things were far worse now, so we siblings left. All the way around the corner into the hall.

Out of sight, but not out of earshot.

"The guy and his family are from..." began Dad.

"Where?" cried Mom.

"Bigfart!" said Dad, his voice exploding.

I swear the sky darkened at that moment. Lightning bolts crashed. Devilish screams pierced the sky. Or so it seemed.

"Oh, have mercy, Lord," said my mom. We peeked into the room to see her sitting on the floor. Her head was resting in her left hand. The shock from the announcement was too much. It was too severe.

"It gets worse! Remember the Hansons?" said Dad loudly. "Not the ones from Saskariver. The Bigfort clan. They have that hockey player kid. Acts like a surfer. Horrible people! Probably. They'll be at our place in an hour!"

"But why did they even agree to come here if they're from Bigfort?" asked Mom, confused.

"To learn our plans and help Bigfart sabotage us!" I stated, bursting onto the scene again. Whoops.

"Joey!" said Mom. "I told you to scram! But since you're here, set the table and prepare things. Get started! I'm going to go lie down for a few minutes."

✹ X ✹

Supper wasn't too awkward for the most part. The dads talked about work, the moms talked about gardening, and their son Ryker and I ignored each other. The subject of hockey was carefully avoided. Best not to have a brawl while vulnerably delicious meatballs were sitting on the table.

I'm not saying we didn't have our moments, however. At one point, my little brother Sam let out a bit of, er, gas. It wasn't subtle, either. It was loud. I looked over at my parents and saw their eyes. They were praying desperately, with devotion and urgency. Their prayers weren't answered.

"That was a BIG FART!" said Sam, smiling like a butcher's dog.

"Like, you're all Saskalosers!" said Ryker.

"Bigfarters!" I said right back.

"That wasn't us; it was literally you guys, dude!" he snapped in reply. "You're the bigfarters!"

"You're the losers!"

"Boys!" shouted four parents at once.

"He started it!" declared Ryker and me simultaneously.

We got through the meal with no more gas attacks and were sent outside after supper. I was supposed to entertain Ryker.

"Want to see the chicken coop?" I asked.

"Nah," he said.

"Horse?"

"Nah."

"Treefort?"

"Nah."

"Dog? Cats? Siblings?"

"Nah, nah, nah."

"What do you want to do?" I asked finally. "Our parents were serious when they said we couldn't play hockey. They know I'll whoop you."

"Cha. I want to do nothing. Like, I hate it here, man," he said.

"Well, boo-hoo!" I said.

"Boo-hoo? Girly dude! How about I take you out with my fists? Then you'll be like all boo-hoo."

"Um." I paused. Getting into a fight with Ryker right now might have disastrous consequences. Like being sent to a boarding school. Or worse, having to miss watching Hockey Night in Canada on Saturday night. I had to think fast.

"*Boo-hoo*, as in...boo! Do you want to see a ghost?"

If you ever need an icebreaker, especially with a sworn enemy you're tempted to annihilate from the planet, just offer to show him a ghost. Nothing brings people together like hunting for disembodied spirits living an unrestful afterlife.

I had Ryker take my older sister Ellie's bike. As we pedaled down the road, I pointed out a few times that he was on a purple bike with yellow flowers. He pointed out to me a few times that he'd bury me alive when we got there.

But the ride was mostly good. At one point, Ryker asked me how our Canada flag day contest went. He knew all about it and was sneering. I told him it was supposed to be a red day, but we decided pink would be different and better. He then told me that Bigfort also decided that pink would be better than red, so that's what they did, too.

What? Now I was flummoxed. How come both towns had their paint tampered with? Did we both sabotage each other in the same way? All these town wars were confusing.

After several more minutes of pedaling, we pulled into the abandoned church's lot and leaned our bikes against two tombstones. From there, I headed towards the church.

"Like, isn't the ghost in the graveyard?" he asked.

"Like, no, it isn't," I replied. "The ghost plays an organ inside the church."

"Uh, dude, you never said anything about organ music!" said Ryker. "Like, let's get out of here." Suddenly, the big, tough hockey player was scared.

"Don't be a baby," I said. I felt brave next to his cowardice.

"Baby! You wanna see what I can do, little homeschooling dude?"

Ryker ducked down into some martial arts pose he must've seen in a movie. His hands were clawing, and his neck bobbed his head to and fro. As I waited for Ryker to pounce, he started making strange cricket noises.

"Like, wheeeee! Ooohh, wheeeeeee! Cha!"

Bigforters are so weird.

I walked past him towards a window of the church. Ryker, dropping his praying mantis pose, followed.

"Step on my back," I said, crouching to my knees, "and tell me what you see."

Ryker boosted himself up using my back as a stepping stool. He peered inside the church.

"What do you see?"

"Like, nothing. Just...."

"What?" I called, his weight taking a toll on me.

"Dude, there's red paint everywhere! Like, I think it might be blood!"

I shuddered. The shudder made Ryker lose balance and fall right on top of me. We collapsed onto the ground.

"Like, oh no! I've got dirt on my tee, man!" he whined.

Ignoring him, I raced to my bike. It was time to get the heck out of there. Ryker followed.

We made it back to my place in under two minutes. Thankfully, it was time for Ryker to leave. That was that. I survived a visit with my Bigfort enemy. He was almost...human? There was nothing to worry about after all.

Nothing, except for the grisly pool of blood resting in the abandoned church.

🍁 X 🍁

"Storthoaks! Speak."

"Yes, Mayor Nutrine. We survived the challenge."

"A miracle!" said Sue Humboldt.

"Pretty much," I said. "Frenchisit, Quebec, celebrated the Quebec flag instead of the Canadian one. They're done." As I spoke, I passed out the usual scorecard.

Saskariver, Saskatchewan
Bigfort, Saskatchewan

Humbleville, Saskatchewan
Whalewatch, Newfoundland
Coolio, Ontario
Womanitoba, Manitoba
Notrudo, Alberta

"What's next?" said Nutrine after a quick glance.

"The next Canadian symbol is the RCMP! The Royal Canadian Mounted Police."

"Police! No!" said Crazy Neighbor. His body pulsed violently. He pulled his cowboy hat down low, covering his face.

"It's okay, yeah," said Mustache. "When we were younger, Crazy Neighbor once hit a homerun. The ball went over the fence and smashed into a police car. He thinks they've been after him ever since. Yeah. He grew a beard right after that incident just to hide. We were only twelve. He's had it ever since. Oh yeah."

"That wasn't me," said Crazy Neighbor, "I'm ten years older than you!"

"Oh," said Mustache. "I must be thinking about my brother and his beard. Cleanface's his name."

"Anyway," I began, taking it upon myself to explain briefly. One must assume that general knowledge was lacking in this particular room. "The RCMP started as the NWMP, North West Mounted Police, in 1873 to preserve peace and prevent crime in the West. They became internationally famous for their traditional red serge uniform and always getting their man, such as the Mad Trapper of Rat River. In 1920, they officially became the RCMP. Their motto is to *Uphold the Right*."

"Okaaaaay," said Lorne. "NWRCPM, er, that's enough alphabet soup for one day there. How about we broadcast all the police calls for a day on my radio station, Hailstorm FM! The best radio station in the North West Mountains of Saskariver, er."

"I'm not sure they'd like that," I said.

"Yeah. We'd know how often they go for doughnuts." Mustache said this while shoving another doughnut in his mouth.

There was a lengthy pause. Finally, Dale Tisdale said what everyone was thinking.

"So...we'll have a doughnut day then?"

"Yes!" said Mayor Nutrine.

"No!" I said. "Insulting the police won't help us win. Besides, *everyone* goes for doughnuts. Not just them. That's a stereotype."

"A type of stereo?" asked Lorne.

"Forget it," I said. "I mean, we need to keep trying to be unique."

"Horses! A musical ride," said Sue Humboldt.

"I'll play only songs by The Police on my radio station. Hailstorm FM! The best radio station..."

"A massive game of cops and robbers!" interrupted Dale Tisdale.

"Against Bigfort, yeah," said Mustache.

"A town gun range! Shooting those beautiful RCMP firearms!" said Crazy Neighbor. "There are crows and magpies and..."

"Stop!" bellowed Mayor Nutrine. "Let's hear what *Joey* wants to do."

Don't you just love being put on the spot? I'd rather be in *jail* than forced to decide such a crucial event and...

"Jail!" I shouted.

"'Jailhouse Rock!' Okaaaaay," said Lorne. "I'll play it all day on my radio station. Hailst...."

"No!" I interrupted. "We'll have a community fundraiser. We'll set up a temporary jail. Then, people can pay to have the police come and arrest other people. I don't know. Fifty dollars to lock someone up for an hour? They can just drop the money off at the police station?"

"I'll be locked away forever!" cried Nutrine.

"Well, we can just do it for one day. And maybe charge two hundred dollars an hour for the mayor and councilors," I said. "People are too cheap around here for that kind of money."

"Okaaaaay!" said Lorne Redvers. "This will be a big police day of jails and money! But where will the money go?"

"We donate the money to the Saskariver RCMP when finished," I said. "They can buy new guns or..."

"Doughnuts," interrupted Dale Tisdale.

"But, what about Bigfort?" asked Sue Humboldt. "How will we stop them?"

"Leave that to me," smiled Mayor Nutrine. Her smile had that evil look about it.

Maybe doughnuts would've been better after all.

CHAPTER NINE

RCMP

"Joey Storthoaks, you're under arrest. Yeah."

I was sitting at my kitchen table on a Friday morning. Believe it or not, I was even doing my schoolwork. *Was*, until a large three-ton Lumber Coop truck pulled into our yard. RCMP was hastily written onto the side of the truck. An eight-foot by ten-foot cage was strapped to the back of the three-ton. And the truck's driver was a clean-shaven man dressed in full police regalia. Officer Mustache.

At first, my mom was annoyed that my school work day was being interrupted. Then she perked up. "Going to jail is like a civics class! But wait...I thought the police were supposed to arrest people?"

"I *am* the police, yeah," said Mustache, munching on a doughnut as he spoke. "They had to deputize us boys from the Lumber Coop. Too many people getting tossed into the slammer today. Almost getting out of hand, yeah."

"Aren't you going to read me my rights?" I asked, hoping for a big production before my younger siblings. I was thrilled that someone thought I was worth fifty dollars!

"You have the right to remain silent, yeah. Anything you say can and will be used against you. Oh yeah. You have the right to a lawyer. And, aww we gotta hurry."

"I'm scared!" cried my sister Rebecca.

"Can I come?" asked Sam.

"Can Sam come?" I asked Mom and Officer Mustache.

"Might not have room. Nope. Yeah," he replied.

I grabbed the town's camera and we went to the truck. Mom insisted I ride in the truck's cab instead of the cage out back. This was disappointing. I wanted to go to prison in style! Oh well. Going to jail was still exciting. The highlight of my week. If only I could go to jail every day. I sang Elvis' "Jailhouse Rock" the entire way.

We pulled into town, past the *BOB'S CUSTOM GLASS* sign—the *GL* had long been stolen—and down the road to the police station. Suddenly, Mustache took a left turn towards the high school.

"Wait!" I said. "Where are you taking me?"

"To the high school, Joey. Yeah."

"What? Why? I want a lawyer. I'll call the police!"

"Look, Joey," said Mustache. "I said things are getting out of hand. The police station jail is full. So, we made another jail at the library. Boy was the librarian, Miss Fancy Spudd, mad! Told all those police and criminals to whisper and all. Yeah. It was so bad we had to drag her away to another jail we created. And this new jail is here at the high school gym. Aww, yeah."

Mustache stopped the truck and hopped out. He opened my door, strapped some dollar store handcuffs on me, and led me inside the high school straight towards the gymnasium.

What a sight! People everywhere. Some were sleeping. Others crying. One young boy was swatting at flies. An old man was swatting at nothing—the prison time making him go coo-coo. There were business owners, seniors, students, parents, entire families. I even noticed Evelyn Carnduff there. She's that girl who's my age. Might go to my church. Might've been at my hockey game. Might've spoken to me at the school draft. Er, um. Let me tell you about the strange noises! It was music, maybe, echoing throughout the dismal air of the jail. And it was loud! Way too loud. This is not what I envisioned prison time to be like. I thought it would be more glorious. More prison-y.

"Okaaaaay," I heard from across the gym.

I looked and saw Lorne Redvers pacing back and forth. The floor was wearing out where he was treading. He was nervous, so I went over to him.

"Oh, hey there, Joey there!" he said. "My radio station, Hailstorm FM, the best rad..."

"What's up?" I interrupted.

"Okaaaaay, so... My radio station there had all of us workers arrested there! No one is playing the good tunes now. Not even 'Bud the Spud' or 'Bark at the Moon!' I hit repeat on just one song there before being dragged away here. Sooooo, that was four hours ago. Someone biggly rich is keeping me here."

"And I have no one working at my restaurant," cried a man a few feet away. "No chicken balls!"

"No mail delivery!" said postman Neil.

"No gas station service!" cried Danny, the award-winning gas station attendant.

"No more school," said teacher Mrs Toeckes.

"No more books," said librarian Miss Fancy Spudd.

"No more Nutrine's dirty looks," said Crazy Neighbor.

"That's impossible!" I said, starting to count vigorously in my head. The numbers were growing faster than the government's national debt, so I used my fingers to help with the carrying and adding. As smoke escaped from my ears, I spoke, "This has to be *billions* of dollars worth of money!"

"Our town is shut down!" said Lorne, his voice rising. "Anything can happen out there now."

I looked about and saw a baby crying in agony. So new to this world and yet afflicted with untold anguish. Meanwhile, a clan of three brothers I knew, Tom, Nate, and Jake, were delirious from the torture.

"We're outdoor boys!" yelled Tom.

"Our dad will kill us!" added Nate.

"I am huuuungry!" shouted Jake, taking a bite out of Tom's left leg.

Shaking my head I said, "Lorne, you didn't..."

"Okaaaaaay," he confessed. "It was an axe-a-dent. I didn't know there."

"Oh Lorne!" I said, fighting back the urge to throttle him. The song was permeating my soul now. Let's just say it was about a girl becoming a Barbie doll in a Barbie world, and...

"Oh yeah. Another load!" trumpeted Mustache, plowing in from the main doors. Two dozen more Saskariver prisoners marched into the gym. Their hands were over their ears. Some were already crying. One of them begged to be handed the death penalty instead.

"Mustache!" I called.

"That's *Officer* Mustache!" he barked back. Power was getting to his head. That or the song.

"Officer Mustache," I called. "I know this was my idea, but be reasonable! The town will fall apart if people can't get to their jobs."

"No time, yeah," Mustache snapped back. "There's a riot downtown I must get to. I'm the only hard worker, you know. Yeah. Those lazy other Lumber Coop police officers. Don't do anything. Nope. Gotta go."

As quickly as he came, he left. The crowd quieted down. Unfortunately, this made the techno-pop beat of the song smash into our heads, like an anvil falling from a canyon onto a coyote's unsuspecting noggin.

"Make noise, everybody!" shouted Miss Fancy Spudd. I'd never heard a librarian say *that* before. "Lalalalala!!!!"

"Lalalalala!!!" screamed everyone else. This wasn't a prison. It was the home of fallen angels. The netherworld.

"Please, help us," I raised my eyes to heaven in prayer.

"Mamma-mia! We have to forgive our enemies! Somehow!" said Father Wally, the local priest, being led into the gym. He, too, had just been arrested. Who next? Santa Claus? All the grandmas from the nursing home?

When the darkness reached its deepest, most hopeless moment, a light broke through. Literally.

Pow! Smash!

The side doors of the gym went flying inward. So, too, did 1,300 pounds of flesh, hide, and bones. We were saved.

"Marty!" I shouted.

Marty the Moose. Our local legend added to his stature that day. He heard the cries and came to our aid, smashing through the door.

Marty gave a loud guffaw, smiled, and trotted quickly out of the gym. Then, there was a mad rush to the exit.

"People!" I yelled. "Take turns! It's o...."

"Okaaaaay!" said Lorne. "Let me go there first there! I need to change that there song!"

Immediately, everyone in the gym backed away to let Lorne through. Priorities.

I'm told Marty went and opened the library jail as well. Prisoners, on the point of unrecoverable insanity, were given new life. Some say Marty saved lives that day. Maybe.

However, as good as Marty was at helping those in prison, he couldn't prevent the mess that was left on the Saskariver streets. There was a major cleanup to do. Chicken balls were everywhere. Library books were strewn out onto the road. Chips from the gas station had been tossed into the street. It was frustrating. It was puzzling.

"Haven't caught who did this yet, yeah," called Officer Mustache, driving by. "It's a mystery."

"Where's Mayor Nutrine?" I asked, holding out my handcuffed wrists for Mustache to unlock.

"Still in the main jail, yeah," he said, pulling out a key to free me. "Marty can't break into *that*. She's been there all day. At least this day has had one good thing about it."

"Officer Mustache, you'd better let her out," I said. "I think this has been enough for one day."

"Oh yeah."

Marty the Moose ran by as we spoke. He was trotting around eating all the loose chips and chicken balls. Just doing his part to clean up the town. I gave him a wave. It made me grateful to have such a protector. A guardian moose. A legend. Just doing his part to *Uphold the Right*.

🍁 .X. 🍁

Joey Storthoaks age eleven reporting for Saskariver.

How are you I'm fine? The RCMP have a motto. "Uphold the Right." Sometimes things don't go as planned. Bad guys (or girls because lets face it girls can be badder than guys) ruin plans. Sometimes a simple bit of fun gets sabatooged and people get hurt.

What do you do when this happens? You Uphold the Right. As you see in my pictures Saskariver had a awesome day planned. But then a nearby rich town that i wont mention (a BIG town with a FORT even though they don't actually have a FORT) had our entire town thrown in jail. But we didn't give up.

A miracle happened. Marty the Moose came to save us all. Then he went and helped clean up our town. And everyone joined in (except the mayor). We worked together to Uphold the Right. If that doesn't make the RCMP proud, i dont no what will.

I hope you vote for us to continue with this challenge i wonder if Marty the Moose would like Moose-Juice? Probably!

Joey Storthoaks,
Saskariver, Saskatchewan

Chapter Ten

Diversity

It's me in the present again. Remember? I'm telling this story while hiding in a closet in the mechanical room of the Saskariver rink. It smells, but not as bad as the dressing room I was kicked out of.

I hear irritated roars echoing from the stands of the rink. Everyone in Saskariver and Bigfort hates me right now. I'm hoping the crowd just leaves, but they'll probably stay until I show my face. I will get booed and hissed. I will probably get run out of town. I haven't felt this bad since I once brought an overdue book to the library and had to pay a fine. Miss Fancy Spudd sure let me have it in a fierce whisper-yell.

In all my waiting, I've been sitting here thinking. That's a dangerous thing. To cheer myself up, I've been thinking about happier times. Namely, Christmas.

At Christmastime my family has a tradition. We do not open presents on Christmas morning. There is no classic waking up at four in the morning and racing down to open the latest Lego present while parents are roused by shouts and excitement. Nope. None of that.

Don't feel sorry for me. We open presents *the night before* instead! Hours before any of you. Take that! It's not bragging, just facts.

"Why?" I once asked my mom.

"Because that's what our families did when I grew up. It's an old French-Canadian tradition."

"Why?"

"Because it's an old French-Canadian tradition."

"Why?"

"Because it's how *we* celebrate Christmas. It's a special thing that developed over many, many years."

So, each Christmas Eve, we kids would pretend to nap, have supper, and get dressed for Midnight Mass. We'd get home super late, have meat pies, chips, chocolate milk, and open presents. I loved it! I still love it. It's a perk of being French Canadian.

Every culture has its perks. One kid I knew would bounce around uncontrollably every year in late January.

"Why are you so excited?"

"It's Robbie Burrrrrrns Day!"

"Who?"

He'd say something like, "O, wad some Power the giftie gie us To see oursels as others see us! It wad frae monie a blunder free us, An' foolish notion."

"Robbie Burns is the Swedish Chef?"

When you're young, you can laugh about that kind of thing. I think the word is diversity. Something like that. People from different cultures and backgrounds living to-gether, more or less happy. It's all good. Almost like a glimpse of heaven. Until the world of adults emerges.

I used to go to real school. Why I left doesn't matter. I still have memories of school, however. Kids were kids. Boys fought, were friends, and fought some more. Teachers were grumpy, were grumpy, and then were grumpy some more. Girls were always evil. But somehow, at the end of the day, we were all friends in our small town. We could play with any other student on any random day. Yes, it was a small glimpse of heaven.

One day, this was ripped from us. We were sitting in science class when a knock came at the classroom door. Our teacher opened the door, and a man from another town stood there waiting.

"I'm here to take my crew for the day," he said. I suppose I need to point out that the man was of a particular ethnicity. I'll leave that vague because it doesn't matter.

"Oh, right," said our teacher. He was blushing. "I forgot about that."

Our teacher called three boys and one girl out of the classroom. Just like that, they were gone. The inevitable questions came.

"Where are *they* going?"

"How come *they* don't have to do the test?"

"Why can't *we* go too?"

"It's not fair!"

Our teacher tried to change the subject to the actual subject of science. But we found out from the students the next day. They were whisked off to the golf course. The day was spent smacking golf balls, eating restaurant food, and having a grand old time. They went several times that year, all during school hours.

Why them? Why not the rest of us? Well, there was a program where students of their specific ethnicity were taken from class to the golf course. That's all I know or care to know. It was the first time I noticed, or at least cared when noticing, if a student had different eyes, skin color, or a different way of speaking. I don't understand why it happened like that. I don't want to understand.

Diversity is a loaded subject. It should be simple in Canada. It isn't. So, let me tell you the next stage of my story. Of how *Canadiana Magazine* threw me into the diversity fire. I wasn't prepared for it, didn't understand it, probably failed it. I bet I'll offend you here. Right? But what's another person being mad at me?

🍁 X 🍁

"Here's the report from *Canadiana Magazine*," I said, passing out the customary pieces of paper with town names."

Saskariver, Saskatchewan
Bigfort, Saskatchewan
Humbleville, Saskatchewan
Whalewatch, Newfoundland
Coolio, Ontario
Notrudo, Alberta

"We made it to the next round!" I continued. "All thanks to Marty the Moose. The magazine loved that part of the jail story. Like it was all orchestrated. Moose. Moose-Juice. A nice touch."

"I'm surprised Bigfort made it," said Dale Tisdale. "I heard they had a mess on their hands."

"More like their hands were in a mess," said Crazy Neighbor. "Good job planning that sabotage, Mayor Nutrine!"

"Huh, uh, yeah! No problem," said the mayor. She seemed confused.

"Finding out about their free handcuff promotion. Then, secretly switching all the keys around. Most of the town was handcuffed, and no one could get out! It was brilliant, just brilliant!" Crazy Neighbor was chuckling as he spoke. "They must be bribing the judges to still be in it. That or the other towns in the contest are really struggling."

"Oh, uh, I'm just full of big ideas," said Nutrine.

"You're a big..."

"Moving on," I interrupted Lorne Redvers before he could say what was on his mind. "We have a challenge that I'm not sure I understand. The next Canadian symbol is diversity."

"No problem there. Hey? I almost went to diversity after high school," said Lorne.

"Sounds like it," said Sue Humboldt, rolling her eyes. "Lorne, *diversity* is including and embracing a range of peoples, backgrounds, cultures, and so on. *University* is a big school you can go to after high school."

"Okaaaaay," he replied, a little confused.

"Canada is a diverse country," I said, trying to explain what I didn't quite understand. "Of course, there are the First Nations, but then the French and British came over. Settlements were made. Treaties. Battles. Kidnappings. Broken treaties. Friendships. Residential schools. The Battle of Batoche. Growth. World wars. Immigration. Internment camps. It's very complicated. Messy, too."

"What are we going to do?" said Mayor Nutrine, not in the mood for a history lesson.

"I guess we show the contest how diverse we are," replied Sue.

The room got quiet. These great minds were thinking. Plotting. Scheming. Finally, the floodgates of ideas and imagination broke through.

"The Chinese restaurant owners are Chinese!"

"Bob here is Ukrainian!"

"A Filipino family lives down the street from me."

"I think we have a doctor in town who's from Africa!"

"Anyone in wheelchairs? Besides the old people at the nursing home?"

"Saskariver has Indigenous residents! We can build a totem pole!"

"Miss Fancy Spudd looks Irish. That should work."

"Mexicans! We need Mexicans!"

"Muslims!"

"Someone without an arm!"

"No. Missing a leg instead!"

"An arm *and* a leg!"

"Swedes are all the rage these days!"

"Guys!" I interrupted. "What? What are you saying? I don't get it!"

"Joey, you foolish little boy," said Mayor Nutrine soothingly—I hated when she talked like this. "It's simple. To be diverse, you only need to set up pictures of people with different cultures and abilities. You make things *look* different. Everyone smiles. Everything is perfect. Everyone is happy."

"I'll book it for Saturday," said Bob Yorkton, the administrator.

"Book what?" I asked.

"The cultural day," said Dale Tisdale. "We'll just have everyone come out. Make them bring their food. People like food. And dress up. Snap a few pics. And boom, we're done!" He said this while holding his hands out in victory.

I knew what they were saying. Like my old textbooks when I went to school. Diversity meant having the right group of people assembled for fake-happy pictures.

"I have another idea," I said.

"Maybe next time, honey," said the mayor.

"It might work, though," I insisted.

"No!" she shouted. This was more like her.

"It's more authentic," I continued.

"Diversity is not about being authentic!" she raged. "It's about using people who look different to get what you want!"

With that, the adults started planning out their cultural diversity day. And I, because of my age, felt excluded. That's diversity for you.

"We'll plan a diversity training session!"

"Send invitations to the Bigfort town council."

"When they don't show up, we'll have someone tell the magazine that their town refused to learn about diversity!"

"Suckers!"

"Racists!"

My mind drifted off. I was in school again, so to speak. And the people around me were golfing. I was miserable.

I must be too young to understand.

CHAPTER ELEVEN

DIVERSITY IN ACTION

I showed up that Saturday, as did all of Saskariver. Spirits were high. Victory was near.

As my family and I walked by the fairground, suddenly, we felt left out. Everyone was dressed up. Everyone but the Storthoaks clan. We dressed as ourselves. I guess that wasn't a very diverse thing for us to do. I'm used to being a little different from others. Sometimes I prefer it. Today, though, I felt uncomfortable. The pressure of being diverse meant I had to go along like everyone else.

"Let's go watch the Ukrainian dancers!" said Mom. "It'll be like dance class for school!" She loved anything to do with dancing. I probably let her down by taking up hockey instead of dance.

We watched. They were good. I enjoyed it. Until I tried to mimic one of those boys kicking their legs out while hovering above the ground, like a rabbit slipping on ice but never falling back on its bottom. I pulled a muscle in my leg. Thus ended my Ukrainian dance career.

"Let's try some Filipino food!" said Johnny.

We ate. It was delicious. Those spring rolls sang to me. Afterwards, my gut sang to the world. The gurgling sound of praise. It's better than the gurgling coming from another part of the anatomy.

"Let's go try the African drums!" said Josh.

We drummed mightily. I hadn't had this much fun hitting something since the last time Ellie and I got into a fight. Celebrating other cultures was a blast. Dance. Food. Song. Well done, Saskariver.

We continued walking along the fairgrounds. We were met by even more booths. Unexpected booths.

"What's that?" asked Ellie, a little surprised.

There was a booth letting people dress like Indigenous warriors. The costumes, however, were violent. Something seemed off.

Another booth had face painting. Kids lined up. However, when they left, their faces were not of different designs or animals. They were different colors. As in, some kids had their faces yellow, others red, some brown or darker. The kids would go back to their parents. The parents looked shocked.

"What the heck?" said Dad. "Who planned this thing?"

"I don't know," I lied. Or was it a lie? I don't remember planning *this*. I felt uncomfortable. I stopped taking pictures.

"Wheelchair races ahead!" shouted Josh. "Wanna race?" he asked, turning to Josh.

"Boys, not now," said Mom. "We might leave soon."

"What's that?" asked little Rebecca.

There was a boxing ring set up. One set of boxing gloves had a Russian flag imprinted; the other had a Ukrainian flag.

On the other side of the boxing ring was a dress-up station. Boys and girls were being invited to dress like Catholic priests and give out crackers to their parents. A pretend Catholic Mass of sorts.

Father Wally was there, pleading with the person running the stand.

"Mamma-mia! No," he wailed. "This is a mockery. Please stop! Heaven help us!"

They weren't stopping. They, whoever *they* were, didn't want to stop.

"We're leaving!" said Dad. He was upset. This whole event was turning out more than weird. It was becoming a chance to make fun of others.

As we turned to go, I saw Mustache. He was dressed as a lumberjack. His face had a panicked look on it.

"Why did you guys do this?" I shouted as I walked by.

"No! Joey!" he cried. "We didn't do *this*! Yeah. We didn't plan these things. Oh no! Yeah," he blubbered.

"Bigfort?" I asked.

A single tear ran down Mustache's kind face, but he didn't reply.

We walked out. A lot of people left. Just like that, Saskariver was limping to the end of the contest. It would take a miracle to save our backs now.

That, or the mind of an eleven-year-old boy.

🍁 X 🍁

Joey Storthoaks age eleven reporting for Saskariver.

How are you? I'm okay. Look. i don't want to write to you. I'm supposed to report about Saskarivers diversity day. We were suposed to show how diverse we are. Like taking pictures of different cultures will make us seem good and Canadian and diverse and yeah.

It was a disaster. There were different cultures and religions and stuff. Some of it was fun. But some of it was mean and making fun of people. I think whatever people live in your town, you need to be kind. Does this make sense?

Im going to change my plan here. Please don't tell Mayor Nutrients. She'd be all mad. Maybe eat all the doughnuts again two. This is what i wanted to do in the first place...

I didn't want a diversity day. I wanted to just send past pictures taken from the town events weve already had. I didn't want it fake or ~~anothentik~~ not real. I just wanted to show you who we are when nobody is noticing. I hope this is good with you?

The first picture is from Beaver Day. See those two kids dressed like beavers and smiling? One of them is Christian. He's a refugee from Eastern Europe. Beside him is Emmy. Mom says she's Jewish. I remember when I went to school that she had autism. They are always welcoming othrs.

And this picture is of Coach Macklin and his family. Hes German. His wife is from Egypt. They adopted two kids from South America. Theyre smiling in this picture. Behind them is Malachi. His family has always been living on this land.

And in this picture are the Chans. They run the Chinese restaurant. Everyone loves them and they love everyone. Here there talking to Jeremiah Santos from the Philippines. The

Chans gave Jeremiah a job when he first came to Saskariver to help his family get started.

And this picture has Father Wally. Hes Polish I think, cause he like perogies. Well i like them to but i'm not Polish. Father Wally is talking to Mr. Garzy who is from France. They were thinking of ways to help a girl from our town who has cancer and needs money to get helpd.

I have many other pictures to show you. They are all of the same thign. A diverse town that doesnt brag about it. A town that is just happy to be Canadian. And I think most of all we have kindness for each other. If the world did this first it would be a better place.

I hope you dont kick us out of the contest. I'm sorry for the trouble we caused. We're not really racists or anything. Bigfort probably is racist. I hear they celebrate something in November called Black Friday. Sounds horrible. But we arent racist.

Joey Storthoaks,

Saskariver, Saskatchewan.

P.S. Moose-Juice is like diversity because there are lots of different flavors. Get it?

It was worth a shot, though not much of one. That was out of my control. I wrote it and felt mostly better. The only lingering question was, if kindness was so important, did this mean being kind to *everyone*? Even Bigfort people?

CHAPTER TWELVE

A SASKARIVER WINTER

"It was a good run, kid," said Crazy Neighbor, turning to me at the town council meeting. I think the meeting was called to decompress and mourn.

"All things happen for a reason," said Sue Humboldt.

"Sad, but we did our best. Yeah," said Mustache.

"Mmmbhlhwp!" said the mayor, chomping on a freshly baked scone.

"It'll be okaaaaaay," said Lorne Redvers. "I will play some happy music there to cheer the town up. On my radio station. Hailstorm FM. The best..."

"Time to get back to normal," interrupted Bob Yorkton.

With the appropriate words said, everyone in the room looked down at their plates. The gourmet treats looked good. They smelled good, too. Within seconds, enormous handfuls of delicious buttery pastry jumped into their mouths.

"We're moving on," I said suddenly. "We're *not* eliminated."

Within microseconds, enormous mouthfuls of delicious buttery pastry jumped from their mouths onto the mahogany table in front of them. Followed by a massive chorus of shocked voices saying one simple word:

"WHAT?!?"

"We, uh, didn't lose," I repeated. "We made it to the next round."

"That's literally impossible!" said Sue Humboldt. "Absolutely inconceivable! Positively implausible!"

"And," said Lorne Redvers, "that there is hard to believe."

"Joey! Don't mess with us! We're old and can't have our hopes dashed. Yeah." Mustache seemed unsure if the news was true.

"Bigfort sabotaged us and made us look racist," said Crazy Neighbor. "There's no way!"

"We moved on," I said. "They sent me notice this morning."

"But how?" asked Dale Tisdale. He seemed the most surprised of all.

At this point, I had a choice. To distract from what happened, or to take full credit. I knew what I should do. Bragging is wrong. Taking credit is not humble. My parents would expect me to do the right thing.

"Well..." I began. "*I* wrote a different letter. And I sent in different pictures. The judges loved it!" Humility isn't my middle name.

"Oh great!" shouted Nutrine. "You lied to them, and now we'll be in bigger trouble!"

"I didn't lie," I said, "I was honest! I told them what happened. The whole truth. Then, I sent in pictures from past events. I explained that celebrating diversity, whatever that's supposed to mean, is more authentic when you *live* it every day. With kindness."

"You did all that?!" said Sue Humboldt. "I'm impressed! I wish my son Xander was like that."

"Well done, young Joey," said Bob Yorkton.

"Yeah."

"Okaaaaay!"

I started blushing. But not because of the good that I did. I was blushing because I gave myself away. I purposely made myself look good. And now I was feeling ashamed for it. Live and learn. I'm eleven. If I'm smart, I'll remember how foolish it all made me feel.

"Anyway, Bigfort moved on as well," I said.

"Impossible!" said Crazy Neighbor. "They were racist for not going to the diversity training! Those racist racists!"

"Actually," said Sue Humboldt, "they *did* show up. I guess they were playing it safe."

"Oh, this cat-and-mouse game is getting deep there," said Lorne. "But we'll outsmart them there. We're smarter! Cause Saskariver is harder to spell than Bigfort, and..."

"Let's just move on," interrupted Mayor Nutrine. "What's next, Joey?"

"The end is near!" I said, passing out the usual papers.

Saskariver, Saskatchewan
Bigfort, Saskatchewan
Humbleville, Saskatchewan
Whalewatch, Newfoundland
Coolio, Ontario

"As you see, there are five towns left. Bigfort, Humbleville, and Saskariver are still going. I think the organizers love our Saskatchewan spirit! The second-last challenge is...the Canadian winter! You know? Forty-below weather, snow, ice, snowshoes, skiing, hot chocolate, frozen feet...the full meal deal."

"But, it's May!" shouted Lorne Redvers.

"June, actually," said Sue Humboldt.

"You didn't let me finish there," said Lorne. "It's, uh, er, *may*be June, is what I was going to say there."

"Whatever!" said Nutrine. "What are we going to do?"

"I was thinking..." I began.

"A ski hill!" said Crazy Neighbor. This opened the floodgates.

"Snowshoes!"

"Bobsledding!"

"Hot Coke! Er, hot cookie! Er..."

"Hot cocoa!"

"Christmas!"

"Santa! Yeah!"

"Presents!"

I drifted off again. Best to let the brains in the room do the thinking. I was ready to go home anyway.

Still, as murmurs and shouts echoed through the room, something was bothering me with this group. Like some*thing* or some*one* was off. Not to be trusted. A betrayer? Like...I don't know. I just didn't feel right. Maybe it was all the buttery scones.

🍁 X 🍁

"You mean I have to dig out all the winter gear! In June!"

"Why? Is that a lot of work?" I asked innocently.

Wrong thing to say. My mom was upset about having to pull out winter clothing for seven children, all for an hour or two of wear. Doing anything times seven adds significantly to one's workload. It must be at least three times harder.

"Please, Mom?" I begged. "We'll see if our winter gear insulates us from the heat or conducts more heat into our bodies. It'll be more science class!"

She sighed. I had her there. We were going to be dressed for the occasion.

The plan was for the Saskariver Winter Festival to be held in the park near the town's water tower. I had an inkling of what to expect but was soon blown away. Saskariver was pulling out all the stops!

When we arrived, snowsuits, toques, mitts, scarves, and sweat were all around. It was a sight. The place was buzzing. It wasn't long before my siblings and I had candy canes and hot chocolate in our hands and sugar in our brains. We started racing from event to event.

"Mom! Can I go snowshoe?"

"Dad! Can we build a snowman?"

"Mom and Dad! Can we join the snowball fight?"

Now I know what you're thinking. Saskariver borrowed some snow-making equipment from the nearby Elk Valley Ski Resort. You'd be wrong. The "snow" was shredded paper. That's right. Tons and tons of shredded paper. It was everywhere.

"Like the snow?" asked Crazy Neighbor as he came over to say hello.

"I thought they'd have real snow," said Dad. "It'd make our snowsuits feel less warm anyway."

"We couldn't rent the machine!" said Crazy Neighbor. "Bigfart beat us to renting the snow-making machine. But we won't let that defeat us."

"Where'd you get all this paper?" asked Mom.

"Uh, you know, this and that..." he answered, a sheepish look on his face.

"This is a *lot* of paper," Mom persisted. "It doesn't just grow on trees, you know!"

"Oh that's a fact!" said Crazy Neighbor.

"Just tell us," I said. "We won't tell others."

"Oh fine! It was my idea! We shredded up some town documents and stuff. We just went into the vault, and voila! There was paper everywhere!" Crazy Neighbor's eyes were shining like a Christmas tree as he spoke. "But that wasn't enough! So, we went to the schools. Students hoard assignments with bad grades so they don't have to show their parents. Let's just say there are a lot of bad marks in this town! Or, were..."

"Wow!" I said, "I wish you'd shredded my schoolwork, too."

"And then Sue Humboldt's law office was very generous with paper to shred," he added. "As was the hospital, nursing home, bank, Lumber Coop, post office, hotel, and Dale Tisdale had a ton of it too. That guy seems to have unending supplies for everything..."

"So, basically, you shredded every piece of paper in town," said Dad.

"Pretty much, yep."

We looked around and saw the enormous "snow" field where people were snowshoeing about, cross-country skiing, or even just lying down making snow angels. Bob Yorkton had some dogs harnessed to a sled, giving youngsters a memorable dogsled experience. Christmas music played, a large bonfire was lit, and a Christmas tree was decorated. The *Grad 59* and *Grad 87* graffiti on the water tower had been covered over, and a large painting of Santa and his reindeer now overlooked the town. But without a doubt, the center attraction was standing *next* to the water tower.

There, nearly as tall as the tower, was a mountain. A mountain right in Saskatchewan! The mountain was covered with paper snow, and kids climbed up with sleds and skis. The pictures I was taking did not do it justice.

"How did you make a mountain?" I asked Crazy Neighbor.

He blushed again, and I knew why. Crazy Neighbor works at the garbage dump. Hauling garbage out of the landfill is a tad bit illegal. Hauling the garbage and piling it into a giant mountain in the middle of a town while having kids crawl up and slide down is a tad bit very illegal.

Suddenly, the Christmas music stopped. A voice coming from bulky speakers echoed out to the town.

"Okaaaaay! Welcome there to winter in Saskariver. It sure is hot here, and so is our chance of winning! See what I did there? Alriiiiiiight!"

If I had to make a wild guess, I would say it was the voice of Lorne Redvers.

"Okaaaaay! Saskariver! Big Mayor Nutrition, er, Nutrients, has been on the road there in her car. She's gone there to ask for a special guest. Please give us your hands to welcome, straight from the North Pole, Santa Nicholas!"

Cheers erupted. The young kids yelled and waved. A large Lumber Coop truck drove slowly onto the scene. On the back deck of the truck, sitting on a majestic red chair, surrounded by Lumber Coop workers dressed as elves, sat the big man himself.

"Ho, ho, ho! Yeah! Merry early Christmas! Aw, yeah!"

Santa started passing out gifts. Screws. Slotted angle brackets. Pieces of lumber and shingles. No expense was spared. This was a winter festival to remember.

"Sure getting hot here! Yeah! Ho, ho, ho!"

It was getting hot. Too hot. But the excitement carried us through.

"Ho, ho, ho! Who wants a pound of inch-and-a-quarter roofing nails? Yeah! Duplex wall plates! Pressure-treated deck balusters! We got it all. Oh yeah!"

Everyone was in a frenzy. Parents were pushing past the kids to the front of the line. It's not every day Santa hands out paintbrushes and drawer knobs. Whoever Santa was. I couldn't figure it out. A very convincing actor, probably. Or maybe the real one?

"Step right up! I've got a premium doorjamb replacement seal! Only for those on the nice list! Yeah! Ho, ho, ho!"

It was so exciting. Too exciting. At least for me. I can't handle crowds like that. Never could, never will. With my eyes still on the Santa spectacle, I drifted away from the crowd.

"Ow!"

Right into someone.

"Sorry," I mumbled, turning to see who it was.

"Oh, Joey," said the figure in a light-blue snowsuit and white toque.

"Oh, it's you," I replied, trying not to collapse in fear.

It was Evelyn Carnduff. Now I was *really* sweating uncomfortably. She smiled at me, so I looked down at her hands. I think she blushed.

"Nice hex-headed sleeve anchors," I complimented.

"Thanks," she said. "Santa gave them to me. He said the three-eighths-inch size was all the rage this year."

"Yeah, my dad has that kind," I said. Then I looked up at her and realized something. I was talking to a girl! "I gotta go!" I quickly added.

"No, you don't," she said, smiling wryly. "You're just trying to avoid *this*."

"What? I planned this day!" I said defiantly. "I'm not avoiding this day!"

"I didn't mean the day," she said. "*This* as in talking with me."

You could've made me run through the crowd in my underwear, screaming the national anthem while holding a large stuffed turtle, and it wouldn't have been more awkward than this moment.

"I think you did well with this event," continued Evelyn. "That's all I wanted to say."

"Thanks," I said, completely in shock. "As long as we beat Bigfort..."

"Oh Joey!" she interrupted. "Why does it have to be about beating Bigfort? Why can't you do your best for our *town's* sake?"

"Because!" I said. "They're our enemy! We hate them!"

"I don't!"

My mouth hung open. Drool spilled down onto my winter gear. My eyes glazed over. She didn't hate Bigfort? What could I possibly say to that? Can you even reason with such delirious people?

"Why *don't* you hate them?" I asked in an angry tone.

"Why *do* you hate them?" she said in a kind tone.

"Because! I told you why! They're the worst!"

"That's fine," said Evelyn calmly. "But they're actually, you know, kind of like us. A small town in the same province. It's the same farming area. And both places have a young arrogant hockey star leading the way."

I paused. Was...that a compliment? Or an insult? Oh girls! They're so confusing. Dad says it only gets worse. And...

"Anyway, thanks for this day, Joey. I love it. Because it's fun for us. Not because it's to beat Bigfort."

With that, she walked away. Evelyn Carnduff. Who was she, anyway? She didn't hate Bigfort! And yet, I remembered, she was always kind to people. Even to a home-schooled misfit like me. Like she didn't have enemies. Or, was it something else? What were those words from the Good Book that Father Wally told me once? Something like, "*Love your enemies.*"

These thoughts were making me dizzy. Hot and uncomfortable. I couldn't take it. I ducked around the fake snow mountain to where I would find some shade. But I didn't find cool relief. What I found was the source of the added heat.

"Fire!" I bellowed. "Fire! Fire!"

The crowds were still mesmerized by Santa. No one seemed to be listening. I ran to the nearest vehicle parked along the street. That of a friendly man nicknamed Green Truck Guy. His truck was unlocked. I jumped in and started hammering on the horn.

No sound.

"Oh for crying out loud!" I said, slamming the door and racing back to the town gathering. Everyone was still focused on Santa Claus.

"Ho, ho, ho! Stain-resistant grout for your bathroom tile! Aw yeah!"

I was going to have to do something uncomfortable. I ran past the Santa truck to where I saw Lorne Redvers talking into his public-address microphone.

"Saint Claus is really giving out the treats there families. Come see Mustache! Er, come and see *his* Mustache! And beard. Cause this here is the real Santa!"

"Mr. Redvers! There's a fire!" I shouted.

"And he's a jolly gut there. Jolly guy. Never wastes a cookie! Okaaaaay..."

I dashed in and ripped the microphone from Lorne's hands.

"Saskariver! There's a fire! Right behind the mountain!"

This got everyone's attention. Eyes bulged. Shrieks pierced the sky. This could get ugly quickly.

"Just calm down!" I urged. "Everyone! Carefully move toward the picnic tables. No rushing!"

What do you know? People started doing what I said!

"Hey! We need to put that fire out! Ho, ho, hurry! Yeah!" Santa was shouting at me. He was right. We needed to get this fire out, or the entire town would be lit.

For now, people were out of harm's way from the fire. That was good. The fire was spreading quickly, though. That was bad. Almost as if there were tons of shredded paper around feeding the flames.

"Call the fire department!" came a shout.

"It'll be too late!"

I looked toward the mountain and saw my answer.

"We don't need the fire department! We need the police department! Are there any police here?" I shouted into the microphone.

Everyone started looking this way and that. Soon, heads started shaking.

"Does anyone live in the houses over there?" I asked over the speaker. "Anyone with guns? We need guns right now!"

"You're crazy!" shouted Dale Tisdale.

"Do as he says!" replied Crazy Neighbor.

Small Saskatchewan towns are filled with hunters. Hunters have guns. Several men raced to their houses across the street. Within ninety seconds, I had a small firing squad at hand.

"Start blasting holes in the water tower!" I yelled.

"What? No!"

"It's our only hope!"

The men paused. Then, one by one, rifles were raised. Finally...

Pow!

"Too high!" I yelled. "Aim for the reindeer!"

Pow! Pow! Pow!

Those poor reindeer on the water tower. Water started gushing from their wounds. Heart shots. Lung shots. Even a few shots to the head. The painted reindeer started splashing gallons and gallons of water. It was a torrent of rain sent from heaven.

Pow! Pow!

More water. This time, someone had taken out Santa himself.

"Oh no! Yeah!"

The water tower Santa, that is. Now, the fire was taking a beating. The paper set to ignite moments ago was being soaked into a white pulp.

Pow!"

"Hey! That's enough!" I called. And it was. The fire was getting crushed. Saskariver was being saved.

As I stared at the scene, the microphone was snatched from my hands.

"Saskariver! Thanks for coming out to the festivities! We'll see you next time. Goodbye now! And remember what great planning your town and mayor have done!"

I wasn't going to steal the microphone back. Not from Mayor Nutrine.

I made a fast exit to where my family's vehicle was parked. Within a minute, my parents and siblings showed up.

"Never a dull moment," said Dad as he saw me. "At least I scored some more hex-headed sleeve anchors."

"Merry Christmas," I replied.

CHAPTER THIRTEEN

A BIGFORT WINTER

"**C**hocolate ganache layer cake! Is that the best we could do here? How about something I can actually *eat*!"

"I'm sorry, Mayor Nutrine," said Bob Yorkton, "I wasn't given much notice to plan this meeting.

It was a special meeting hastily called after the Saskariver Winter Festival mishaps of that same day.

"Besides," continued Bob, "I had enough trouble getting that water tower patched and the park cleaned up. I'm only human!"

"I demand a lot," said Nutrine, "because that's how I get re-elected." She stared down at the cake in front of her and sighed. "Would somebody take this away from me and get me something edible? Some French palmiers and lime seltzer?"

I looked at the clock. My bedtime was in thirty minutes. She'd better hurry with this meeting.

"While we're waiting, we may as well talk about why we're here," said the mayor. "The time has come where we put our heads together and devise a plan to take down

Bigfort. We've been letting them off the hook. It's time to crush them!"

"Here, here!"

"Ho, ho, ho...yeah!"

"Okaaaaay!"

"So," continued Nutrine, "we *all* need to participate. All of us! Tomorrow afternoon they have an event. From the Bigfort news release, I see that those copycats will have a winter festival. At the park near their rink. Have you all read their planned events?"

"Yes," came the chorus.

"All of you must have a sabotage plan. Don't worry about getting caught! You'll all be wearing winter clothes anyway. They can't see through scarves and toques! Let's start with Crazy Neighbor and then go around the room."

"Well," said Crazy Neighbor, "I know the Elk Valley Ski Resort folks. They come to the garbage dump with old ski lift chairs and stuff. Those chairs make great lawn furniture! I've sold a bunch of 'em for a pretty penny! I, uh, anyway. The snow-making machine is already in Bigfort. I've told the Elk Valley guys I will run it for them. They're happy to hear that. And..."

"You're helping them?" shouted Mayor Nutrine.

"No! I will dye the snow as I blow it. No white snow! I can do whatever colors I want. Pink! Purple! Whatever. It'll be hilarious!"

"Yellow snow!" said Mustache.

"Excellent!" said the mayor. "And you, Mustache?"

"Uh, they're supposed to have a special guest show up at the event. I imagine it'll be Santa Claus. Yeah. So, I'm going to try to do some stuff with that. Maybe swap their candy treats with rotten tomatoes. Yeah."

"Or this horrible chocolate ganache layer cake!" said Mayor Nutrine. "Where's my palmiers? On second thought, maybe just some Italian white Alba truffle! And you, Dale?"

"Well, they're firing their ice-making machine up for a real hockey game. I'll sneak into the ice machine room and turn it off. Let the ice melt. By the time they figure it out, they'll be playing in a pool!"

"Perfect!" said Nutrine. "Lorne?"

"I got some new, uh, speaker system stereo-types there, uh. So... I'll just blast the music to other songs instead! I'll play some of that there Hawaiian music instead. Something like Melekalimikamaameka, er, okaaaaay."

"Love it!" said the mayor. "Sue?"

"I figure we might be in trouble if we are caught. I'm going to be snooping around, looking for ways to, um, uh, convince them that it would be in their best interest to let us go. Uh..."

"You mean blackmail them?" I asked.

"Yeah," she said. "I'll see what I see. You know. If they build a mountain out of garbage from the dump, they could be in legal trouble. Stuff like that."

Crazy Neighbor winced.

"A bit lame, but necessary, I suppose," said Mayor Nutrine. "Who's left? Bob!"

"I already took it upon myself to sign up for a food vendor stand," said Bob Yorkton. "I'm going to be selling burgers!"

"You're fired!" yelled Nutrine.

"Reindeer burgers! It'll freak out all the little kids!"

"You're hired!" yelled Nutrine. "And that leaves young Joey here. What are you going to do?"

All eyes turned on me. I squirmed. This did not make me feel comfortable. Not just the eyes staring but the fact that we were sabotaging others. I didn't like what Bigfort was doing to us, but my conversation with Evelyn was still fresh.

"It's an eye for an eye," said the mayor, as if reading my thoughts.

"I'm, uh," I started. I honestly had nothing to say. Nothing! "I'm going to have a plan for tomorrow. Yeah! You'll see!"

"That is *unacceptable*!" said Mayor Nutrine, her eyes glaring at me.

"What about you?" I snapped back without thinking.

She looked shocked. Her nose twitched. Her belly growled.

"Meeting adjourned!" she said. "Good luck tomorrow. Or else!"

🍁 X 🍁

My parents weren't thrilled that I was being picked up after Sunday Mass.

"Sunday is our family fun day!" said my mom.

"You mean forced family fun day," I said. "I've got places to go."

"He's going," said my dad. "We didn't know it was going to be like this, but we can't have Joey start something and not finish it. Just this once. Though why they need him, I don't know."

So, it was settled. I was to leave for Bigfort after Mass.

At the church, it's safe to say I was distracted. My younger brother Sam, at one point, jumped up onto the pew, turned around to face everyone—we sat up at the front—and started doing a disco dance I had taught him two days earlier. He did this for a good minute and had everyone laughing. I didn't notice until my mom hissed at me to "*stop him!*"

I also didn't notice when someone posted the wrong hymn number. So, the choir started singing the words and tune to one hymn while the congregation sang another.

"Let there be peeeeeace on Earth..."

"Onward Christian soldiers..."

"And let it beeeegin with meeeee..."

"Marching as to war...!"

At least it wasn't a Christmas hymn this time. Not that I was paying attention. My mind was on my impending sabotage mission. What if Sue Humboldt didn't find any blackmail protection? Would I be thrown back in jail? And was it right to do this anyway? I mean, morally speaking.

Finally, I received some Divine assistance. It came from Father Wally's sermon. At first, I zoned out. But he sneezed twice, starting coughing, and then an altar boy threw water in his face. This got my attention. I started to listen.

"My beloved," he began calmly, water dripping from his face, "today's words are most necessary. '*Love your enemies and pray for those who persecute you...*' What could be more difficult? Yet, what could be more rewarding?"

Not these words! Anything but these words! Father Wally continued.

"I sometimes wonder why things are so confusing in life. Why do we fight so much? What if we *didn't* fight? We might just get a glimpse of peace. A feeling of harmony. Just a glimpse. Like a mustard seed. A piece of heaven. We must nurture this. If not us, then who?"

He was giving me plenty to think about. But Sam started doing another disco dance. And that's the last I remembered of church that morning. That and one of the altar boys fell asleep, started snoring, and then got dragged out by his angry mom.

Soon, Mustache and the gang picked me up outside the front church doors, and I was on my way. The mood in the vehicle was tense as we drove. Our winter gear sat on our laps as the fields and trees passed.

"I still haven't figured out which color to make the snow!" said Crazy Neighbor in a panic. "I was going to mix some colors, maybe. But what if I mix them wrong, and they come out white?!"

"That's impossible," said Sue Humboldt. "And at least you have a plan! I'm supposed to find something *while* I'm there! What if I don't?"

"Then I guess we go to jail. Again," I said.

We pulled into Bigfort and parked far away from the hubbub. After putting our winter gear on and taking out all necessary supplies, we walked towards the festivities.

"Time to split up, yeah," said Mustache.

"Okaaaaay! Good luck," said Lorne. With that, we split.

I waited a long while. I didn't like this. What if we didn't always fight? Would there be a glimpse of something better?

Finally, I started wandering around. I had to admit, Bigfort was vibrant this day. Like they brought their A-game. My first stop was at the food stands. There were pastries and hotdogs, fried chicken and corndogs. One of the food stands, however, had a significantly longer lineup. Walking over, I read the sign:

SANTA'S REINDEER CUISINE
Blitzen Burgers - $9
Rudolph Onion Rings - $6
Prancer Pizza Pie Slice- $7
Donner Doughnuts - $2

"Like, this is hilarious!" said a girl my age, walking away from the stand. "It's, like, like we're eating reindeer!"

"Blitzen's delicious!" said a girl beside her.

"Well, Mr. Yorkton failed," I muttered quietly.

I decided to check out the hockey game at the rink. It was probably a local exhibition match-up. Walking into the rink, the familiar cool feeling hit me, which was nice, seeing as I was dressed for winter.

"GOAL!" shouted a crowd of spectators.

Sure enough, Ryker Hanson had his arms in the air while doing a lap around the very-much-intact ice. He must've scored the goal. Probably his tenth of the game. That guy was getting in valuable summer practice on me! I left the rink. Dale Tisdale didn't do a very good job of sabotaging the ice. Another fail.

Walking around, I spotted Sue Humboldt. I was going to go say *hi* but decided not to. She looked dejected. Clearly, she was failing at her job.

I went to the main attraction. There was supposed to be a ski hill in place with real snow. This ought to be good!

The music was pumping out loud and clear. It was Hawaiian sounding alright. Lorne had done it. He'd got his music to play throughout Bigfort. Catching the words, they went:

Here we know that Christmas will be green and bright
The sun to shine by day and all the stars at night
Mele Kalikimaka is Hawaii's way
To say Merry Christmas to you

This song was familiar. Of course! I'd heard a version of it before by old-time singer Bing Crosby. It was about Christmas in Hawaii. Looking around at the crowds and the vibe, I don't think I could've picked a more perfect song. It fit the mood without blemish. Another fail. Oh Lorne...

The ski hill came into view. Santa and his reindeer had been painted next to the giant BIGFORT letters on their water tower.

I was hit with a surprise as I approached. The snow wasn't white! It wasn't hot pink, orange, or neon yellow, either. It was green and red.

"This is amazing!" said a mom to another lady.

"I know, right! Christmas colored snow! We're sure to win! We're so smart!"

A massive failure. We were helping them win. We were literally helping Bigfort to win. Our only hope was Mustache.

"Ho, ho, ho! Yeah!"

A team of horses came rolling onto the scene, pulling a fancy red sleigh. There were several sacks on the sled and a jolly man dressed in red and white.

"Come here for some gifts! Yeah. Ho, ho, ho!"

It had to be Mustache. Right? No one else in the world says *yeah* after each phrase. Right? Yeah?

"Look, Mommy!" cried a kid. "I got ten packs of hockey cards!"

"I got a new Barbie doll!" screeched a girl.

"I got a new cordless impact driver!" cheered a man.

This was getting ridiculous! Why would Mustache be helping Bigfort win? Was he betraying us? Was *he* the one I had that bad feeling about earlier? My heart sank. I was confused. Mustache was one of my few friends. He wouldn't do this, would he? No. I had to have faith in him. Even if this trust was the size of a mustard seed. So, I looked suspiciously at what was before me.

Santa was passing out treats and toys. But his belly looked a little hollow. His voice was less trumpet-y and more tuba-y. His movements were a little forced. And his eyes... I did not like the look of his eyes!

"You're not Santa!" I said loudly.

"Who said that?" someone growled.

"Hey, kid, leave us alone!"

"Don't tell our kids it's not Santa, you creep!"

"This is NOT Santa!" I shouted again.

I looked up at this Santa; he was glaring at me. Finally, he spoke up.

"Alright, kid! Let me show you something! I can be just like Saskariver! Yeah!" With that, he pulled out a gun.

No, you heard that right. Santa pulled out a gun. I'm not joking. The crowd gasped and backed off. Santa held out the rifle for all to see.

"Take a look at this! Yeah!" Santa pulled the gun into position, locked the bolt in, and fired.

Pow!

It was Violent Night. Jingle Bell Glock. Blast Christmas. Shouts and cries resounded. Water started splashing down from the water tower.

"Just like Saskariver! How's that for you? Ho, ho, ho! Yeah!" said Santa before kicking his horses into gear and galloping out of the park and out of view.

"What just happened!"

"Mommy, I'm scared!"

"Santa has a gun!"

"Run, Rudolph, run!"

On went the screams and shouts. I was so confused. Mustache couldn't have done that. Could he? No. I had to believe in him.

I backed away from the scene. Good thing, too. It was turning into bedlam. Water was splashing onto the snow, melting it away. Soon, rivers of dyed red water, like blood, were drenching the feet of the Bigfort residents. Children cried. People slipped and fell. Curses were heard. Their day *had* been sabotaged. We did it after all. Or, someone did anyway.

An hour later, I was back in the vehicle, driving home. Mustache wasn't with us. I asked where he was.

"Not here," was all Dale Tisdale said. His face was tense. "Yeah," he added for good measure.

❧ X ❧

Joey Storthoaks age eleven reporting for Saskariver.

How are you? i'm fine. Our Saskariver Winter Festival was a hit! Nothing was spared in our work to win the challenge. Not even our water tower. We didn't have real snow. But we made snow. I think these pictures will show you what a great day it was.

Someone keeps starting fires at our events. i'm conserned and i'm also worried. But if you let us do the next event, I think youll be amazed. I promise you it will be good! Moose day! Time for are secret weapon. Do you think my writing has improved. Mom says its getting better?

Gotta go! Gotta go get more Moose-Juice that is! Haha.

Joey Storthoaks

Saskariver, Saskatchewan

P.S. I'm worried that I haven't seen my friend Mustache. I don't know why I'm tellin you this. But I'm a little scared.

SANTA'S REINDEER CUISINE
BLITZEN BURGERS - $9
RUDOLPH ONION RINGS - $6
PRANCER PIZZA PICE SLICE- $7
DONNER DOUGHNUTS - $2

Chapter Fourteen

Moose Day

Here are the "minutes" from the following town council meeting:

- Mustache wasn't at the meeting. Mayor Nutrine said he was on vacation.

- Dale Tisdale explained that the police were searching for the Bigfort Santa.

- I announced that Saskariver made it to the next round, as did Bigfort and Humbleville. Coolio, Ontario, and Whalewatch, Newfoundland, were eliminated. They both made the massive mistake of playing Mariah Carey's "All I Want for Christmas Is You" song on repeat. There were mini-riots.

- I also reported that the next Canadian symbol was the moose.

- The councilors agreed to order Marty the Moose's favorite cake and bribe him to visit.

There was a general unwillingness to do anything further!

- Mayor Nutrine said she was getting her nails done that evening, and so the meeting was adjourned.

I love Marty the Moose, but I felt like we were being overconfident in him. Besides, Dale Tisdale kept saying that Humbleville was very good with their events. Shouldn't we try our best? And *where* was Mustache?

Sigh. I guess I should tell you about Moose Day.

🍁 X 🍁

Moose Day. Time for Saskariver's secret weapon.

As usual, I went to town with my family. The event was held at the fairgrounds. The weather was drifting in between clouds, rain, and sunshine. Mediocre weather to match the mediocre vibe.

There wasn't much for events or excitement. Lorne Redvers had some music playing. Mostly songs by the 1960s band called The Archies. My dad said there was an Archie Comics character named Moose Mason. It wasn't the cleverest idea I'd ever heard. But it was better than when Lorne would announce after each song, "Alriiiiight! Who wants to hear more *moose-ic*?"

We walked to the main grandstand. At the stage was a large table. The table held a massive...something covered by a cloth. Beside this were a set of moose antlers and a sizeable horn, which I knew was a moose call.

The music stopped, and Lorne Redvers took to emcee-ing the event.

"Okaaaaay! Saskariver! We're at the end there of this here event! Just we'll win this here challenge and then it's the finals!"

A few drops of rain fell. Lorne got nervous. Flustered even.

"I see it's going to rain on us now. Hopefully, our cake surprise under the cover here, er, it's not a cake, but a sur-prise that's not a cake... Er, hopefully, the not-cake doesn't get wet too much, so we can not eat the not-cake and not have, er, Marty come..."

Mayor Nutrine walked up on the stage and grabbed the microphone from Lorne. She then stared fiercely at the clouds. The rain stopped. Not even the weather messes with her.

"Saskariver! It's Moose Day! What better way to cele-brate than to have our local celebrity stop in? Let's call out Marty!"

With that, she waved her hand to the cake. Lorne rushed over to pull the cloth from the large "not-cake." As Lorne pulled, everything started tipping over.

"Lorne!" screamed the mayor.

Crazy Neighbor ran onto the stage to steady the sur-prise. Then he and Lorne pulled off the cloth. It was a mas-sive cake with white icing and blue trim. Marty's favorite.

"Okay, Marty!" said the mayor. "Come on out!"

Cough

Ahem

Cricket chirps

"Marty!" she called once more. "We have your favorite food. Cake! Now come on out and show the world that Saskariver has Moose-Mania!"

Still nothing. I had that sinking feeling.

"Don't just stand there looking like two idiots!" she shouted at Crazy Neighbor and Lorne. "Call him!"

Lorne grabbed the large moose antlers and started rattling them around, making as much noise as possible. Crazy Neighbor had the moose horn and bellowed the most mournful call I'd ever heard.

"Buurrrr Roarrrrrrrrrrbbb. Erh. Erh Errrrrrrrhb."

Still no Marty.

"Guys!" I shouted from the crowd. "It's best to call moose in October during the rut."

They didn't hear me. Or, they didn't want to hear me. They kept on calling.

"Burrrr Ruuurrrrree. Erh. Erh. Erh."

This wasn't a pretty sight. Mayor Nutrine was blushing mightily. Which made it an extra unpretty sight.

"We need a moose!" she snapped at Lorne and Crazy Neighbor.

Everyone was watching. Our hopes of winning the contest were fading with each passing second. Those poor guys didn't know what to do. So, they panicked.

Crazy Neighbor picked up the cloth from the ground and wrapped it over his entire body. Then he reached out and grabbed the moose antlers from Lorne.

"What is he doing?" asked my dad.

"I don't know," I said. "Wait... Oh no!"

Oh yes. Crazy Neighbor was down on all fours, pretending to be a moose. He started bobbing up and down, stomping and stumbling. Lorne was nabbing pieces of cake and feeding them to Crazy Neighbor. It was quite the show.

"Stop eating the cake!" said the mayor.

"You wanted a moose!" said the moose.

Crazy Neighbor waddled his antlers from side to side. This was too much for the mayor. She wound up her leg to kick the moose in the rear end. As she swooped her foot forward, she slipped, landing on her own rear end. The loud thud from her fall shook the stage. The table buckled, and the gigantic cake slid off, landing right on the mayor.

"Ahh!" she screeched as the crowd laughed. "This is not amusing!"

"No. That there is a-moose-ing!" said Lorne Redvers.

Meanwhile, Crazy Neighbor was still wandering around as the moose. He didn't see Nutrine or the cake—the cover still over his eyes—and slammed into the mayor. Suddenly, the two of them were a mess of cake and antlers.

If I know Marty the Moose—the real moose—I know that it's at *this point* he would make his entrance. Marty is a legend, after all. But he didn't come. No Marty.

While everyone laughed at the scene on stage, my eyes drifted away in worry. Where was Marty the Moose?

I scanned the trees and lilac bushes near the grandstand. Was he hiding? Was he just being too patient?

Looking through one clump of bush, I saw a dark shadow lying on the ground. A big shadow. Roughly the size of Marty. The lump didn't move. It was lying there. Looking like a... Do I have to say it?

Looking like a dead moose.

"Is that Marty?" I shouted, pointing to the bush.

The crowd murmured in shock. Dale Tisdale was nearby and ran over to the bush. After a quick look, he turned to the crowd and shouted.

"It's a dead moose! Marty is dead!"

❧ X ❧

Joey Storthoaks age eleven reporting for Saskariver.

How are you? Im okay. We had a Moose Day. Marty didn't show up. Or at least he didn't show up alive. I saw his body near the grandstand. When i shouted it out the whole town went crazy. There was crying. Kids we're scared. Parents upset. The mayor got mad at me. Don't shoot the messanger! Or the moose! The whole event didn't turn out so good.

We tried. i'm not going to lie and say it was the best event but we tried and doesn't that count? At least i have a fun picture of Crazy Neighbor pretending to be a moose

I guess I'll just leave it in your hands. I'm so sad about Marty.

Joey Storthoaks

Saskariver, Saskatchewan

P.S. Maybe if Marty had Moose Juice he'd still be alive. Oh Marty! I miss him!

❧ X ❧

Two days later, I sat at a town council meeting. There was still no Mustache. Did he *really* go on vacation? Was he dead? Like Marty? I was nervous.

"This sauce stains! I told you not to order sauce that stains my clothing!"

Mayor Nutrine was hitting the barbecued ribs hard. How can people eat at a time like this?

"Joey!" she bellowed.

"Well, uh, so this past week's challenge had us..."

"Just cut to it! What's involved in the final challenge?" she asked.

"The final challenge?" I said, a bit confused. "The final challenge is a combination of all the other challenges. Towns have to show all seven previous Canadian symbols."

"What?" exclaimed all the adults in the room.

"We have to do *everything* again?" asked Bob Yorkton.

"Not at all," I said.

"Can you just make a report about the previous ones and..." said Sue Humboldt.

"The *Canadiana Magazine* is supposed to send judges to the remaining towns," I said, interrupting her. "They will judge *in* person."

"Oh no!" said Bob Yorkton. "So, we have to do all this again!"

"No! You don't have to do any of this again," I said. This was getting confusing.

"Then, what will we do?" asked Crazy Neighbor.

"Yeah," said Lorne Redvers, "how are we supposed to win there without doing something there?"

They didn't understand it. Not at all. I just had to say it.

"Because the contest is over!" I said with loudness, bitterness, and anger. "There will be *no* final round. Humbleville has won! Bigfort and Saskariver were *both* eliminated."

"NO!!!!!" shouted everyone.

"Bigfort, too?" said Dale Tisdale, a slight smile on his lips.

"Both of us!" I said. "Guys. We spent so much time focusing on Marty the Moose and beating Bigfort that we forgot the main point. We put all our moose in one basket and..."

"What?" said the mayor.

"We didn't have any *Moose-Juice* for our Moose Day! The main sponsor! Neither did Bigfort! They were so intent on calling in their own live moose. To beat us. It's like we were so focused on each other that we both lost sight of the goal."

"Oh no!" sobbed Crazy Neighbor.

"Oh yes!" I said. "We're done. It's over. After all that."

Truth be told, I was fighting back sobs of my own.

Chapter Fifteen

The Final Challenge

How does one return to normal after a whirlwind two months? After an emotional roller coaster ride with highs, lows, more highs, and a final crashing low? If you're an eleven-year-old boy like me, the answer is simple: you mope around.

I was feeling sorry for myself, being a jerk to my siblings, getting beat up by my siblings, snapping at my cats, and getting attacked by my cats. Even Doggy growled at me just because I went and hid in her doghouse! It was like being in love and then breaking up. Not a slow drift away either. A sudden break, with all its pain and trauma. Okay, I'm just guessing. I have no idea what *that's* like, nor will I ever. I'm never falling in love and getting married. Never!

I think Mom wanted me out of the house. She said, "Get out and leave us alone!" while adding a few colorful adjectives. But I'm not supposed to say those words.

I hopped on my bike and started pedaling down the road. The wind smashed into my face, the added breeze making me work harder, expending my anger. I biked until my lungs were breathing hard. Which is to say, I biked to the abandoned church.

"What now!" I shouted as I arrived. "Where are you? Murderer! Creep! Clown! You don't scare me!"

I stomped right up to the church's window and lifted myself using my bike as a prop. I was standing precariously on the seat as I peered through the window pane. What came into view was unexpected.

I saw buckets of paint. Paintbrushes, too. Next to these buckets were large containers. Some of the containers were open, and materials and uniforms were showing. A big red uniform or costume was there. And papers. Lots of papers. Signs. And, under a canvas cloth, what looked like chairs. Bigger than chairs. Wheelchairs? Scanning farther back, near the old sanctuary, I thought I saw a rifle case. And beyond it was spilled paint. Or was it blood? The paint, or blood, had thick, coarse hair mingled into it. The hair was short and dark. Dry. Dramatic.

And then I knew. I knew it all.

I flew back home to my writing paper. There were two letters to write.

Dear Mayor Nutrition,
I have a plan. I think i can get us back into the contest. Hold on tight. Order some more donots. We might need another meeting soon.
Joey

And I started the other.

Dear Canadiana Magazine,
It's Joey again. Joey Storthoaks from Saskariver.

There has been sabotage. I can PROVE it. Let me explain...

And I *did* explain.

❦ .X. ❦

"I think I speak for everyone when I say this better be good!"

Mayor Nutrine was wondering, like everyone else, why I had summoned them to a special town council meeting. Sue Humboldt looked concerned. Crazy Neighbor seemed interested. Mustache...well, he wasn't there again. What a time to take a vacation.

"It is!" I started. "We need to get together and..."

"I mean, this dulce de leche ice cream better be good!" interrupted the mayor. "Bob's been slipping lately with his catering choices. But sure, you'd better have something good to report, too!"

"Yes!" I continued. "We need to plan for the final *Canadiana Magazine* challenge!"

"WHAT?" shouted everyone. Mayor Nutrine started choking on her ice cream and needed a drink from her bottle of raspberry-infused imported sparkling water to calm her system.

"We have been reinstated," I said, "because there's been some sabotage."

"*You think?*" said Bob Yorkton sarcastically.

"Yeah, I do," I said. "More importantly, so does the magazine. They agree that something strange is going on. So, we're allowed back in the challenge!"

"That's awesome, young Joey!" said Crazy Neighbor.

"It's just us and Humbleville and..."

"Amazing there, yes, sir!" said Lorne Redvers.

"And Bigfort," I concluded.

"WHAT?" shouted everyone for a second time.

"Well, they've been sabotaged too, apparently."

"Really?" said Mayor Nutrine, trying to look innocent.

"Whatever," I said. "The point is there will be a final round. *Three* places. We must create something incorporating *all* Canadian symbols into one special event. And this time, the judges visit."

"I don't think I could organize all seven in one shot!" complained Bob Yorkton. "I'm only human!"

"Zip it, Bob," snapped the mayor. "If you don't like it, you can return to flipping burgers and making milkshakes at Burger Queen. Joey, what are the symbols again?"

"Beavers, hockey, the flag, the RCMP, diversity, winter, and moose."

"That's like a code we need to figure out," said Sue Humboldt.

"I know!" said Crazy Neighbor. "We'll open a zoo for beavers and moose. The zoo will be like a jail for them. The keepers can be from the RCMP. We'll throw snowballs at the moose, and the beavers can feed on wooden hockey sticks, and..."

"If we do that, I'll throw you in jail," said the mayor.

"So..." said Lorne Redvers, "we could have a radio station segment there. A moose will talk with a beaver.

They'll tell people where to find some hockey snow, er, for diversity, uh…"

"What about a play?" said Sue Humboldt. "A Mountie will be out in the cold, fighting off beavers and moose, going through snow and hockey rinks until he rescues some people in wheelchairs and wraps them up warm with a Canadian flag?"

"We were better off with Crazy Neighbor's idea," said Mayor Nutrine.

"Thank you," said Crazy Neighbor.

"And Crazy Neighbor's idea was as bright as a black rock in the bottom of the ocean," she continued. "Come on now! Think!"

"Ahem…"

"What? Oh you, Joey. Speak now! This is all your fault anyway."

"Well," I began, "I remember how my hockey game against Bigfort ended in a tie back in April. It kind of started this whole thing. What if we played that hockey game again?"

"How does a hockey game show all those symbols?" asked Sue Humboldt.

"Well, Bigfort can be the Beavers; we'll be the Canadians and have a large red maple leaf jersey. We'll be playing a hockey game on ice, like winter, the winners will get presented with a trophy by the RCMP, just like they do in football, and…"

"Brilliant!" said Sue, cutting off my speech.

"Okaaaaay!" said Lorne.

"Let's do it!" said Crazy Neighbor.

"You mean we'd have to fire up our ice-making machine!" said Dale Tisdale.

"That's a lot less work for me," said Bob Yorkton.

"You're missing something," said the mayor coldly. "How in the world would we get Bigfort to agree to come here and help us out? You're nuts!"

"I was thinking about that," I said, "and it fits in well. If the two towns work together, it will be impressive. There's no way Humbleville could win. But it would also mean two different places were working together. We'd involve others who don't get along with us or are not like us. It'd be real diversity in action."

"Wow!" said Sue. "The kid's a genius."

"No, I'm not," I blushed.

"If Bigfort is working with us to beat Humbleville," said Mayor Nutrine, "how do we know who wins the challenge? Bigfort or Saskariver?"

"Easy," I replied. My mind drifted to Ryker Hanson, to goals scored, taunts made, and bodychecks thrown. "It'd be a winner-takes-all game. If we win, we're crowned champion!"

"And if we lose?" said Sue, holding her breath.

"We won't," I said.

❦ X ❦

Bigfort agreed.

At first, they didn't. It was Ryker Hanson who changed the mind of the Bigfort planning committee. He made an impassioned speech that they wouldn't—couldn't—lose the hockey game. He said things like, "Cha, I could beat Joey Storthoaks with my hands tied behind my back and my hair covering my eyes!" and, "Like, that little dude has got nothing on me," and, "Like, yeah!"

So, it was set for Saturday night. The Saskariver rink had its ice-making machine fired up. Coach Kevin Zeigelgansburger had us all come out for practice the night before. It felt great being out on the ice again. The sounds of pucks ricocheting off plexiglass, blades carving ice, and screams of, "Skate faster, you punks!" piercing the air brought me to a place of comfort. The hockey rink is where I can be me, whatever that means. I can play, create, and not notice the world around me.

I'm not saying I wasn't nervous, however. Quite the opposite! I couldn't eat any supper before the game. The weight of having the entire challenge, with all its bragging rights, and cash prize, placed on me was a heavy burden. If I didn't outplay Ryker Hanson, we were done. Not only that, but our rink *needed* the winning money for upgrades. We needed a new roof and possibly a new ice-making machine. Oh the pressure.

I arrived in the dressing room, sure that being around my teammates would loosen me up.

"Joey!" shouted the boys. "Don't mess up, and we'll win!"

I smiled faintly and started getting my gear on. Shin pads? Check. Elbow pads? Check. Cat? Not this time. Skates? Check. New Saskariver Canadians sweater? Check. Camera? Check.

That was a mistake; I shouldn't have brought it with me. I guess it was becoming a habit now. I had been taking it everywhere. To town. To the rink. To the old abandoned church. It sure came in handy with the church, I must say.

"Pass the puck to Joey!" said Coach Kevin. "Don't let the Bigfart parents distract you. Their Saskaloser chant is getting old anyway. And Joey? Don't mess up!"

"Coach?" said our goalie.

"What?"

"I don't feel good. I think I'm going to throw up..."

Chapter Sixteen

The Good Ole Hockey Game?

J ust like that, we were down our goalie. Coach Kevin's son took over. This wasn't the start I'd hoped for. We would allow a goal every time Bigfort took a shot now. However, something else was bothering me. Something far worse. But I couldn't put my finger on it.

We started heading for the ice. The music was pumping. It wasn't our familiar "Chicken Dance" song. It was that tune about a girl being a Barbie doll. My mind started drifting farther away from the game...

"Announcing the Saskariver Canadians!" cried Lorne Redvers over the sound system. "Let's get going there, boys! And win this here game against Bigfart there!"

"Hey!" shouted a Bigfort parent to Lorne. "You can't say that as the announcer! You wanna go?"

"Oh no you guys don't!" called the referee. "Any more of this, and I'll throw the crowd out. Again!"

The parent shut his mouth. You don't mess with referee Ron Spitballer.

There was a ceremonial puck drop. Mayor Nutrine, holding a microphone, walked out onto the red carpet at center ice. She had with her a well-dressed man and woman who apparently were the *Canadiana Magazine* judges. The two had been in Humbleville the day before and said it was "pretty good." I took that to mean the winner of this game was going to be crowned champion. You don't become a champion by being "pretty good."

I was called out to take the ceremonial faceoff against Ryker Hanson. If you're unfamiliar with this tradition, the idea is to have an important person drop the puck. The home team's captain "wins" the draw, picks up the puck, and everyone shakes hands. How nice.

I'm not the captain of my team. I was confused. Mayor Nutrine handed the microphone to the man, and he started talking.

"Ladies and gentlemen of Bigfort and Saskariver. We have Ryker Hanson and Joey Storthoaks here to take the faceoff. I insisted young Joey take the faceoff. We've been so impressed with his pictures and essays and, may I say, private investigative reporting. We would not be here tonight without Joey Storthoaks!"

The crowd cheered politely. I blushed deeply. Ryker snarled angrily. When the puck hit the ice, Ryker swung the puck back hard. He not only won the draw—against *The Code*—but he knocked me down in the process! The Bigfort crowd started laughing. The Saskariver crowd started protesting. Ron Spitballer started threatening. It was time to get the game started before another riot broke out.

The real opening faceoff went. Within five minutes, Bigfort was winning 5-1. Our goaltending was awful. Same with our defense. Our forwards weren't much better. What I mean to say is that Ryker Hanson was outplaying us. Badly. His extra practice from the Bigfort Winter Festival was a sizeable advantage. I should've known this! Never leave extra practice out of your calculations.

Coach Kevin screamed and threatened. I tried harder. The harder I tried, the worse I did. Like I was melting into the ice, unable to move forward. Unable to explode. I couldn't do anything right. Like my mind was distracted. Like something was *missing*. At least the Saskariver crowd was on my side.

"Joey! Win!" shouted my dad. "Or you're walking home!"

"Joey! Why can't you just do your best?" yelled Evelyn Carnduff.

"Joey! You're letting the town down!" bellowed Mayor Nutrine.

I just couldn't play better! I was tanking at the worst possible moment.

"Goal! Bigfart!" shouted Lorne Redvers into the sound system for what seemed like the tenth time. Eleventh, actually. This was becoming one of the lowest moments in Saskariver's history. All thanks to one Joey Storthoaks.

By the end of two periods, we were losing 11-4. Down seven goals! With twenty minutes to play. Unless a miracle happened, we were done.

"Joey, what's wrong with you?" shouted Samson Hanson inside the dressing room.

"Hey, none of that from you!" Coach Kevin told Samson. "Joey, what's wrong with you?" he asked, turning towards me.

"I, uh," I said. "I just can't get going on this ice."

"Well, it's the same ice for both teams! Do better!" he said.

The buzzer went, referee Ron Spitballer blew his whistle, and it was time to leave the dressing room and head onto the ice. As we were walking towards the ice, I looked up at the crowd. Some of the Bigfort crowd were pointing and laughing at me. Others threw trash my way. At one point, I dodged a bottle of Moose-Juice coming at my head.

"Moose!" I shouted. "Moose! I forgot moose!"

"What, Joey?" said my coach. "Get out on the ice."

He wasn't ready to listen to my pleading. I scanned my eyes for anyone nearby who could help me. Standing near enough was Dale Tisdale.

"Mr. Tisdale!" I shouted. "I forgot about moose!"

He lowered his eyebrows in confusion.

"Moose!" I said, hoisting my hockey gloves over my helmet, trying to make them look like moose antlers. "Get something to do with moose, or it's all over!"

Dale Tisdale stared at me. Then he had his *aha!* moment and gave me a thumbs-up. I smiled. This was it! I'd figured out what was bothering me. Now, to erase a seven-goal deficit against a team led by Ryker Hanson. All with twenty minutes left to play and the stakes higher than a mountain.

Perfect.

The puck dropped. I swooped hard at the little disk of rubber. Ryker fell. I skated past both defensemen, stick-handled a perfect quadruple deke, and lined up at center ice to do it again.

That first shift, I scored three goals. Ryker got mad and slammed his stick. It broke, and a shard of lumber hit Ron Spitballer in the ankle.

"Ow!" he yelped. "You sawed-off little runt! Get in the penalty box before I throw your entire team out!"

I scored another goal. Then the coach took me off for a rest, and Ryker scored. I jumped back on the ice and scored two more. It was 12-10 now, with less than ten minutes to play.

"Joey! More!" yelled my dad.

"Keep going, Joey!" shouted Evelyn Carnduff.

"Keep going *or else*, Joey!" bellowed Nutrine.

"Yes!" I said. I was feeling it. Like we couldn't lose. Like everything I touched would turn to gold. What could go wrong?

During the next faceoff, I slashed at the puck. So, too, did Ryker Hanson. We both fell over in a splash. Ron Spitballer blew his whistle.

"Both of you little punks get two minutes for giving each other the business!"

"Dude!" said Ryker.

"Not a word!" said Spitballer.

We were trapped in the penalty box. Soaking wet. I looked out glumly. The clock was ticking. There'd only be six minutes left in the game when I got out of the penalty box. And where was Dale Tisdale with some moose stuff? And...why was I soaking wet? I groaned loudly in frustration.

Father Wally was working the penalty box door. I thought he'd be upset by my latest penalty. Instead, he looked at me gently and said, "Mamma-mia, Joey! You have brought enemies together. In some small, little way. A heavenly surprise! I will pray for you!"

He knelt to pray. This was very kind of him. Unfortunately, the penalty ended, and he was too busy praying to open the door.

"Excuse me!" I said as I jumped over Father Wally, over the penalty box door, and landed on the ice with a splash.

Ryker Hanson was out before me and already had the puck on his stick. I decided to let him weave in and out of the other players, and instead, I skated directly toward my goaltender. As I arrived on the scene, Ryker was already winding up for a slapshot. I dove in behind my goalie. The puck sailed past the goalie's outstretched glove towards the top right-hand corner. It never made it.

Plunk!

It hit me. Right smack on the head. The puck landed in front of me. I shook my head to clear the cobwebs and took off.

Ryker already had his hands up in the air after he shot. I ripped down the ice with the puck before he could even think of catching me.

Water splashed. The puck didn't slide well. But onward, I skated. For my life. For my town. For all that is good and holy. I approached Bigfort's goalie. There was no way I could do a quadruple deke. Not with the ice the way it was. I wound up for my own slapshot.

Ting!

Off the crossbar, it rang. Off the crossbar and down, right into the net. A perfect shot. 12-11!

The crowd cheered! It was chaos. We were one goal away from tying the game. And with only five minutes left to play.

After high-fiving my teammates, I went to center ice to take the next faceoff. Ron Spitballer wasn't there.

"Drop the puck, zebra!" said Lorne Redvers over the sound system. "I mean, er, uh, it looks like there's a delay there or something..."

Spitballer was by the scorekeeper's box. He was talking with the game officials. He then waved Mayor Nutrine over. He also pointed to the *Canadiana Magazine* judges and waved for them to come.

"This can't be good," I said, standing at center ice.

"It's, like, so amazing," said Ryker. "We're winning, so yeah. Cha."

"But we scored the last goal!" I shouted back. "And we're whooping you right now!"

He replied by punching me in the head. I *almost* retaliated. I didn't, though! Thank goodness, because the ref had just turned to see me.

"Boys! To your benches!" shouted the ref. "Or I'll have you thrown out of school forever!"

"This loser's homeschooled," said Ryker. "And, like, I *want* to be thrown out of school forever, cha."

"Go!" shouted Spitballer.

We sat and waited. Finally, the female judge from the contest spoke on a microphone.

"Attention everyone. Something seems wrong with the ice surface. It's melting. The ice-making machine must not be working. We've decided to take a break and try to fix it. If it can't be done, well... We came here for a *hockey game*.

Not finishing the game is like cheating. Plus, I'm not sure where the moose symbol is. No, no, it's too late to just go buy Moose-Juice. I don't know. If this ice isn't fixed, Humbleville will win the contest!"

The two teams were directed to go wait in their dressing rooms. We walked back over the slush to get off the watery ice surface.

Groans rang out. Curses, too. It wasn't pretty. Everyone was tired of *this*. Tired of waiting. Tired of disappointment. Tired of a rivalry that would never end, could never end, didn't know how to end.

"Of course! Typical Saskalosers."

"Oh go have a big fart!"

"If it's not fixed, *we* win the game!"

"No! You cheaters!"

"You're the sabotagers!"

"It's you!"

"Dummies!"

"Yeah? You're so dumb, you sit on your television and watch your couch!"

"Whose idea was this, anyway?"

"That Storthoaks kid, remember! Number nine!"

The frustrations boiled over. Everyone needed an outlet for all the disappointment. They needed a punching bag. And they had one. Soon, I found myself being booed as I crossed the ice to the dressing room. By everyone. Both Bigfort and Saskariver folks. I was the cause of *this*. The booing soon turned to heckles.

"Storthoaks! You suck!"

"I hate that kid!"

"Little punk! Too good for everyone!"

"Can't fit in!"
"Always causing trouble!"
"We don't need him."
"We don't want him."

CHAPTER SEVENTEEN

THAT ESCALATED QUICKLY

It's me, Joey Storthoaks. I'm not speaking in the past tense anymore, or whatever it's called when you tell a story that already happened. I'm here, in the present, and it's tense. It's the present tense. I'm hiding for my life.

Maybe I'm exaggerating a little bit. But not too much. Things are bad. The teams left the ice, or what's left of the ice, and went to the dressing rooms. My teammates started chirping at me. Even my coach joined in. Told me I couldn't put the puck in the ocean. Told me every goal I'd scored this year was because his son had done all the work. Told me he'd replace me with a little girl from the figure skating club next year. So, I told him I'd take my gear and go elsewhere. Let's be honest, I was forced out.

I fled the dressing room, dragging my hockey bag along, and ducked into the maintenance room. It's a dingy old place where they park the Zamboni—the tractor-like machine that resurfaces and cleans the ice. The room has tools hanging and loud machines running. Besides the small entrance door, there is a closet and two massive doors for the Zamboni to drive through. One big door leads to the ice surface. This one is closed. The other leads outside to the trees and field near the Saskariver fairgrounds. This one is open. In other words, I could sneak out and run for my life if needed.

I entered the maintenance room, looking for a place to sit. But as I entered, I thought I heard something! So, I hid right inside the small storage closet. And I've been here since, telling my story to you. I'm hunched over, sitting on my hockey bag. I've taken my skates off and am in my street shoes. I am alone.

Do you feel sorry for me? I don't blame you if you don't. I've made a life of stirring a rivalry, of being an outsider, of not caring what others think, of being difficult. Everything falls apart when I try my best, like an old cookie that crumbles when held. But here I am. In the present. Waiting for something.

Waiting. Praying. Lamenting.

There is a noise stirring from inside the maintenance room! I can see into the space through a wide crack by my closet door. It's Dale Tisdale and Bob Yorkton. They've come to stare at the ice-making machine. I decide to hold my position.

"I don't know why it's not working!" says Bob. "Every time we come back everything looks fine! Maybe it's just this one knob here? I dunno!" Bob lifts a small lever to the *on* position.

"It's more sabotage!" says Dale.

"Well, this sabotage will have me begging for my old job at the Burger Queen pretty soon," says Bob. "Nutrine's mad!"

"Everyone's mad," says Dale. "They can't stand that Joey. Don't blame them, either."

The two leave the room, and I sigh. This is the end. As I wait, I pick up my camera stashed in my bag. I rotate it around. It's cold in my hands. This camera. My pride. My curse. It almost saved me once. Should I tell you how? Would it be bragging? No, I'm not going to do that. Maybe I've learned my lesson about bragging. Besides, what do I have to brag about right now?

There's another noise. I crouch low, though I don't really have to. It's Dale Tisdale again. He's walking in quickly. The door shuts. He's muttering.

"Stupid machine. There."

I watch him walk over to the ice-making machine. He stands in a way that blocks my view. However, I know he's doing something. He's messing with the machine. Not in a good way, either. Dale laughs as he walks out.

And just like that, I understand. I understand everything. It all makes sense to me now. What I don't understand is what to do about it.

I slip out of the closet and towards the ice-making machine. I decide to turn that knob upward.

I hear another noise as soon as I step out into the open room. It's too sudden! I can't make it back to the closet! My only option is to make a break for it.

I run outside the big door. Right into the outdoors. With my head down, I run. Right into what feels like a wall.

"Oof!"

"Ow!"

I hit someone. A shadowy figure. A solid person. Someone hiding out in the woods right behind the rink. I'm scared.

"I'm sorry," I say.

"That's fine," the person says, before adding, "yeah."

"Mustache!" I shout before quietening my voice down. "What are you doing here?"

"I'd ask you the same thing!"

"Where've you been?" I ask.

"Oh...no place in particular. Nope. Yeah."

"I haven't seen you in over a week. People are saying you were the evil Santa in Bigfort. I don't believe it! Are the police after you?"

Mustache looks nervous. He turns his trumpet voice down two notches. "I *wasn't* Santa. Yeah. It wasn't me. They *think* it was me. I've been framed. All I remember is I was in line to get a reindeer burger at the Bigfort winter day and Dale Tisdale came up to me. Told me that people suspected me of stuff. I thought it was because of the pinkish paint shipment from weeks ago. Yeah. Anyway, I snuck away. Didn't want to take a chance. Later, I learned the Santa there was pretending to act like me! To sound like me, be generous, and everything. Yeah. Well, they're after me. I had to take time off work. I've been hiding out. Waiting for things to cool down. Just couldn't resist coming to the game though. Oh yeah."

I'm about to ask who the Bigfort Santa was but more footsteps come from the mechanical room of the arena. Both Mustache and I peer inside while remaining hidden from view.

"The machine is just fine!"

It's Mayor Nutrine. She has the two magazine judges with her. And there's Dale Tisdale and Bob Yorkton.

"Look!" says Bob. "It's just this knob here that keeps slipping down! Ridiculous. Flip it up! Hold it with tape or something. Let's get on with the game."

"You'd better hurry," says the female judge. "We aren't staying here forever."

"And your crowd looks like they're about to rip this rink apart!" adds the male judge.

"Fix it, Bob!" yells Nutrine. "You stay with him, Dale! The rest of us are going back. I need to sweet-talk this crowd. Thankfully, I'm so good at it. And Storthoaks left! Just like that kid. Starts this mess and takes off."

I blush. Mustache pats my shoulder.

Now Bob and Dale are alone again. Bob is puttering around with the knob.

"We could probably take this apart and see why it's not connecting properly," says Bob. He twitches as he speaks. Memories of flipping burgers for a living are burdening his mood.

"Uh, I think something else is the problem," says Dale quickly.

"I doubt it," says Bob

"Is too," says Dale.

"Is not," says Bob.

"Is not," says Dale.

"Is too," says Bob.

"See!" says Dale, triumphant at last.

Bob is confused for a second or two.

"Look," intervenes Dale, "you go find Lorne. He's good at taking things apart. The three of us should be able to find out what's wrong. I'll start while you're gone."

Bob huffs but leaves. The door slams as he walks out. Dale springs into action. He rips at a panel attached to the ice-making machine. It comes off, and he stares blankly ahead at wires and gears, deciding what to do.

He walks to the wall and picks a snow shovel from a tool rack. He strides back to the open panel. He's searching for something. A target.

Dale pulls the shovel back and starts to thrust it forward. I know what he's doing! He's trying to destroy the ice-making machine.

"Hey!" I shout, jumping into the room before his shovel can crash down.

Dale nearly drops the shovel in surprise. When he sees it's me, he carves a smile.

"I'm just trying to get this thing back together," he says.

"No, you're not! You're trying to sabotage it!" I yell. "You're sabotaging everything!"

"Hey, brat!" he snaps. "It's *you* who's been doing this. That's who!"

"That's ridiculous!" I say.

"You think they'll believe a snotty little boy like you over me?" he sneers.

"Yes," I reply, holding up the camera that's been in my hands the entire time. "Especially if I've been taking pictures of everything!"

I snap a picture of him holding the shovel. Dale's eyes bulge. He looks scared. I keep talking.

"I have pictures of you here touching that switch. I've got other pictures! *You* know what I'm talking about!"

"That's literally crazy!" shouts Dale. "I'm a free citizen!"

"You're not actually from Saskariver!" I say. "You only moved near our acreage recently."

This is too much for Dale. He bolts towards me, grabbing my shoulders.

"Give me that camera!" he shouts. His hold is tight. It hurts. "Or I'll smash *you* instead! Maybe I'll smash both you and the camera! And the ice-making machine! And everybody! And... And..."

"Not today!"

Mustache dives in and tackles Dale. He hits hard, and we all topple over in a heap. Dale releases his grip on me and turns to punch Mustache.

"Ow! Yeah!" cries Mustache.

I jump out of the pile and turn towards the melee. I can see that Dale is the stronger of the two. He immediately pins Mustache down and starts feeding him lefts and rights. It's not pretty.

I jump on Dale, but he flings me off, and I hit my head on the ground. Dale jumps up, leaving both Mustache and me in a pathetic pile. He reaches for the shovel.

"First the machine. Then, your camera. Then both of you!" he shouts. "Then I slip out of here. Ah-ha-ha! A piece of CAKE!"

He heads toward the ice-making machine and lifts his shovel in preparation for what will come: a slashing of the town's hope of winning. A sure victory for Humbleville.

Before he can do this, I hear a snort. One I immediately recognize and welcome. And I know why.

"Piece of cake, hey!" I yell at Dale before he can swipe at the machine. "CAKE!" I say again, pointing in his direction.

Before he knows what's what, Marty the Moose comes tearing in! Not a ghost moose but the real Marty, in the flesh. Marty plows through the open overhead door and makes straight for Dale. Dale takes a swing with the shovel at Marty and connects, hitting the moose right on the snout.

"Marty!" I scream.

Marty gives a mournful cry and bounces back, angry. Dale winds up to take another swing. I run towards Dale and throw all my weight at him. He swats me away like a fly, and I go sprawling on the floor. As I crash down, the small door opens, and Bob walks in with Lorne.

"Okaaaaay," says Lorne, altogether flummoxed.

"What the?" says Bob.

Marty spins around and lowers his head for a charge. He's aiming at Dale.

"Open the door!" I cry.

I point to the button that opens the large overhead door leading to the ice surface. Bob hits the switch, and the door starts rising. I can hear a voice as it rises. It sounds like one of the judges addressing an angry crowd through the sound system.

"Seeing as there is no moose and no hockey game, I am forced to dis…"

The crowd erupts in curses and shouts. Never mind that. Where I am, an angry moose is charging towards Dale. Dale dives out of the way just in time. *Ole!* Marty misses, but his moose-momentum carries him forward. The door is open just enough now, and Marty rides his momentum into the arena. He lands straight on the ice and starts sliding. The crowd looks on in shock as a moose crashes the party.

"To disqualify the... What the moose?"

Marty slides to the center ice and stops where the judges and Mayor Nutrine are standing.

"Well, now!" says the female judge. "That's a moose!"

I'm tempted to run into the arena, but I notice Dale Tisdale backing out of the mechanical room towards the outside. He doesn't get far. He's met by Mustache. More specifically, he's met by Mustache sitting on the Zamboni, blocking the outdoor exit.

"Out of my way, yeah!" shouts Mustache.

Dale spins back, trying to exit through the small door. I jump in his way. Lorne and Bob do as well. Dale looks back and sees the Zamboni approaching, hunting him down like a moose ready to charge. Dale's only escape is to exit the main overhead door, which leads out onto the ice.

He turns and runs. Mustache follows. They're on the ice now—Dale slip-sliding along while Mustache powers the Zamboni's motor and yells, "*Ole!* Yeah!"

Dale panics and slips. He lands on the center ice with a splash. Marty comes over and nips at his ear.

"Ow!" yells Dale.

Revenge is sweet.

"What *is* going on?" asks the judge with the microphone. She looks over to the Zamboni entrance. Everyone in the crowd follows her eyes to where she's looking. And all eyes land on one eleven-year-old boy standing there.

Me.

CHAPTER EIGHTEEN

AND THE WINNER IS...

"It's him!"

"It's Joey Storthoaks!"

"He's the one that caused all of this!"

"Mamma-mia!"

The crowd starts yapping at me. Sensing things will get out of hand, the magazine judge starts speaking into the microphone at center ice. Marty and Mustache are there as well, guarding Dale.

"Come here, Joey!" she calls. "Let's have this out right now."

The crowd gasps. I walk out, still in my hockey equipment and shoes. I am face-to-face with Saskariver *and* Bigfort.

"So..." begins the judge. "I see we have a moose!"

Then she does something I dread. She hands me the microphone. Not me. Not shy me! The misfit of misfits. People are waiting. Expecting. And I must deliver.

"Uh, yes," I begin. "We have a moose. It's Marty. He's not dead! That dead moose was planted in the bush the other day. By someone here! It was planted by..."

"No!" shouts Dale. Mayor Nutrine tells him to zip it. So, I continue.

"Dale Tisdale!"

The crowd murmurs. The news hits like a lousy electrician standing in a tub of water. Very shocking.

"Dale Tisdale planted the moose!" I continue. "He killed it over by the abandoned church on *his* property. And more than that, he's been hiding all sorts of things there. Things to sabotage our town. *Both* of our towns!"

As the crowd roars, Dale shouts, "Not true! You can't prove anything."

"Actually, he can," says the male judge, taking the microphone from me. "Young Mr. Storthoaks sent pictures from the old church. A whole pile of pictures. Of paint from the town's flag ceremony. Of moose blood and fur. Of every supply you've ever used. Even a red Santa outfit. This young lad has reported it all. We weren't sure, so we came here to check. We gave Bigfort and Saskariver a second chance, too."

"Joey!" shouts Evelyn Carnduff.

I blush. Why are girls so...caring? Ugh.

The rest of the crowd is in a frenzy. People are shouting out, asking why and how. I am handed the microphone.

"Dale Tisdale sabotaged Bigfort and Saskariver. He lit all the fires. He was Santa over in Bigfort. He's even been shutting off the ice machine here. I have pictures of all of it. The reason is simple."

A hush settles over.

"Dale Tisdale is actually from *Humbleville*! This is all part of Humbleville's plan!"

It is bedlam. Pandemonium. Insanity. I speak quickly.

"Dale's our neighbor in the country but rarely around. He inherited property nearby and somehow got himself on the town council. But he was actually born and raised in Humbleville. And he's clearly very loyal to them."

Dale is sullen now. He sees Sue Humboldt in the crowd and knows that anything he says will be used against him in court. He shrugs his shoulders and waits for what is to come. Meanwhile, I hand the microphone back to the female judge. What happens next is embarrassing.

"Thank you, Joey! This wouldn't be possible without him. What a joy to see these two feuding towns brought together today. What unity! What diversity! Like enemies who chose kindness over hate. And now they have a real moose. Let's hear it for Joey!"

Embarrassing doesn't even begin to describe it. I am applauded long and hard. A standing ovation. Mustache. Coach K. Evelyn Carnduff. Mayor Nutrine. Even Bigfort residents. The whole works. But secretly, I sort of enjoy it.

Finally, things settle down. The judge continues.

"There is only one way to settle this contest. Can someone fire up this ice-making machine and let us finish the game? Winner takes all!"

Bob gives a thumbs-up. Dale is carted away by the RCMP—thus adding to our presentation. Marty heads outside through the large door leading past the mechanical room. And Mustache cleans the ice with the Zamboni. After another delay, the ice freezes enough, and we are ready to continue the game.

🍁 X 🍁

"Goal!"

It's Lorne Redvers on the sound system. I just scored. Just as time was expiring, I stole the puck from Ryker Hanson, did a *quintuple* deke, and buried the puck deep in the net. A real buzzer-beater! It's a tie game.

Ryker slams his stick. The referee, Ron Spitballer, wants to give him an unsportsmanlike conduct penalty. Bigfort's coach starts pleading with Ryker to stop arguing. Meanwhile, I am waiting at center ice for the puck to drop to begin overtime.

I set my stick down. It splashes water upwards. I look around. Sure enough, there is more water. Not this again.

When the dust settles from Ryker's outburst, everyone looks down at their feet.

"What the heck!" says Ron Spitballer. "Who stole the ice?"

Bob runs from the mechanical room and shouts, "It's done this time! The old machine couldn't keep up with the heat and all the starts and stops!"

"Okaaaaay, alright," stammers Lorne Redvers. "Well, there... We have a problem there. Alriiiiight."

After more murmurs and curses—more curses than murmurs—the *Canadiana Magazine* judges are back at center ice with the microphone.

"The ice-making machine is down for good..." says the female judge. "BUT, this time, you boys *did* actually play a full sixty-minute hockey game. And there was a moose!"

She hands the microphone to the other judge. He continues.

"Never mind! We've seen enough. Bigfort and Saskariver, we've decided! It is my privilege to announce the winner of the *Canadiana Magazine* contest! The most Canadian place in Canada! And the winner of two hundred and fifty thousand dollars for community improvements and two truckloads of Moose-Juice is…"

"What? Yeah."

"Okaaaaay, what?"

"What?"

"The winner is…" begins the judge.

Chapter Nineteen

The End

"T he winner is..." continues the judge, "it's a TIE!"

The crowd gasps. I nearly fall over. Ryker Hanson does fall over. After all that... We tied!

"Prizes are to be split. What an honor! What a privilege!"

"What a crock!" shouts Mayor Nutrine.

"Mamma-mia!" says Father Wally from the penalty box.

The crowd is silent.

I walk over to where Ryker Hanson is standing. After all we've been through, all the pain and glory, all the lessons I've learned, I...stretch out my hand to him.

"Good game," I say.

He stares back. Then he smiles. "Cha," he says, holding his hand forward. We shake.

Both communities stare at us, trying to process it all.

"Good job!" cries Evelyn Carnduff. Seriously. Doesn't she know I have brothers and sisters watching? Girls. Ugh.

"Mamma-mia!" says Father Wally again.

Other people start finding their voices.

"Well, it's not the *worst* thing ever."

"And half of two hundred and fifty thousand dollars is a lot of money."

"Okaaaaay! That's like a hundred or so thousands of money there!"

"You know what? This has been fun, too!"

"Good job, Bigfort."

"Good job, Saskariver."

"Good job, Joey!"

And with that, the crowd rises to their feet as the ice pools a little more. They put their hands together. It starts with clapping. Then cheering. Soon, it is a roaring ovation for the ages. Bigfort and Saskariver, together. United enemies. A miracle. A moment of peace. A piece of heaven.

❦ X ❦

I am at home. An unopened Moose-Juice in my left hand, a pencil in my right. I am writing one final letter.

Dear Canadiana Magazine.

I sit here with my Moose-Juice in hand, writing a letter of thank you. First of all thanks for the Moose-Juice! the town decided to give me half of the truckload as a thank you.

Thank you also for the share of the prize money. Saskariver is going to get a new ice-making macheen and even patch some of the rinks roof.

And thank you for challenging our towns. Weve had a hate for Bigfort that has gone on for years and years. Every single part of this contest had us trying to beat Bigfort. But in the end, I think we learned something. Bigfort is just like us. They have boys who play hockey, mayors who try to put on a show, and people who like to cheer for where they come from.

Don't get me wrong. I still hate Bigfort! But...i dont really hate them. Does that make sense? They are rivals, but I think when things get down and out, they are also on our side. I think what I'm trying to say is, sometimes we shouldnt take others, or ourselves, quite so seriously. Like we're all in this together. Like it's importanter to live in peace than constant anger.

Sincerely,

Joey Storthoaks,

P.S. Please don't show anybody this letter. I don't want them to know I said this!

My fingers crack open the Moose-Juice. I walk to the kitchen sink and start pouring it down the drain. Horrible stuff. Not fit for drinking. I wouldn't even make Ryker Hanson drink it. But I smile. When I cash in the bottle deposits, I will be a rich, rich eleven-year-old.

I walk outside. The day is warm. Inviting. Peaceful. One of those rare moments I am learning should not be taken for granted. They don't last forever. Life goes on. The world still turns. With its wars, sicknesses, even rivalries. But enough of that for now. There is a time and a place for everything.

I head over to the large bucket leaning next to our house. It is full of sports equipment. I pull out a hockey stick and tennis ball.

I am thinking about my town's feud. How it went. How it brought people together. I think of Ryker. He's a good guy. Cha. I think of our rivalry. How, if we keep it in check, it makes us better. Forever rivals. But with a new respect.

I am content. I am at peace.

I walk over to my hockey net, leaning against the side of our old shed. It is time to practice. It is time to get better.

I start hammering slapshots.

Ping! Ping! Ping!

Hockey season is only two months away! I have a tie to overcome.

And as everyone knows, a tie is like kissing your sister.

THE END
LEAVE A GREAT
AMAZON REVIEW!

ACKNOWLEDGMENTS

My wife and children: Yes, "Dad wrote another book." And still, you don't look down on me too much. Thanks for all the love and support.

Small town Saskatchewan: You're the quirkiest, weirdest, most unusual whatever there is. And I love it. I also fit right in.

My editor, Shavonne Clarke: I hope my ritings gotten gooder. Thanks four being the best editer!

Brent Butt and Corner Gas: For all the inspiration and laughs.

My launch team: Without you, I'd just be some idiot sitting in a basement. But thanks to you, I'm an idiot sitting in a basement writing books. Your support is greatly appreciated!

All the students I've ever taught: If it was up to me, I'd fail you all! Just so I could teach you again.

The Good Lord: Deo Gratias!

A MISSION FOR ALL

O h boy, things got nasty. The words were leading to shouts, screams, and pushes. A stuffed chicken got thrown on the ice. Followed by a Bigfort parent. Followed by an actual chicken. In the end, Ron Spitballer threw the crowd out of the game. That's right.

"Everyone out!" shouted Ron. "The game doesn't continue until *everyone* goes and leaves a positive Amazon review for this story!"

"Like, not fair, man!" shouted Ryker Hanson.

"Not fair!" stormed Ron Spitballer. "*Not fair* is enjoying yet another story and not supporting the author! You sawed-off little runt! Why don't you go leave a review, too!"

I looked on as nearly two thousand people spilled out into the night. Soon, all that remained was a single cat sitting in the stands. It was Catman.

"You too!" said Ron to the cat. Catman drifted off to the exit, her tail between her legs.

One by one, the crowd returned.

"Hey, leaving a review was easy!"

"Sure was! Took half a minute!"

"And it helps the author make more stories!"

"You see," said Ron Spitballer, as the arena filled with people once more, "I'm not a heartless son of a gun after all!"

He turned to center ice and blew his whistle hard.

"Now, you little brats! Let's start this game again before I throw you all off the planet!"

Bonus!

You will not want to miss other books in the *Adventures of a Misfit* series!

I present to you an excerpt from *My Rocky Mountain Challenge*.

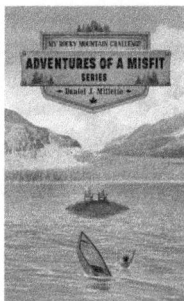

We walked inside. Then we groaned. This wasn't good.

It turns out that Sulphur Mountain has four peaks. The red chairs were all the way at the fourth peak. To get there involved real-deal mountain climbing. Like mountain climbing for experts. Lest you end up as poor Philip Stanley Abbott at Mount Lefroy in 1896. Tumbling down like a rag doll. Not pleasant.

"So," stammered Mom, "how are families supposed to get to the red chairs from here? Are they trying to kill us? Is that what this is about?" Her voice was escalating.

"No, not exactly," said Dad. "Just kill our wallets. Look over there. By the big windows. That's a rental place."

"What do you rent?" I asked. "Red chairs?"

"I wish," said Dad. "You rent mountain guides. I mean, you pay for someone to guide you along the mountain's ridge. And you pay to use all the safety equipment, helmets, and harnesses. I'll bet you pay per person. Hundreds of dollars per person."

"I don't like this," said Mom.

"Well, is this it?" I shouted. "We're done? After getting to six chairs!"

"It would be in the thousands of dollars, Joey," said Dad. I could see he was shocked and disappointed.

I stormed outside the interpretive center and walked down the path for a minute. The sky was clear, and the view was stunning. Banff was something. Imagine building a town in the most outstanding place you could find in the Rockies. The founding of the town of Banff was something like that. What did it matter? I'd always remember Banff as the place where my dreams were shattered.

I must've been grimacing as I stood looking down on the town because an older couple strolling past stopped to say something.

"You groovy?" asked the man. He had a massive head of gray dreadlocks, a tie-dye shirt, and baggy orange shorts. I'd say he was a hippy if I didn't know any better—an honest-to-goodness hippy. I'd never seen one before in Saskariver.

"I'm good," I lied.

"Forest," said an old lady in a hemp hat, long white dress, and rainbow necklace, "I think he's just chilling."

The man, apparently named Forest, nodded. "Got it, Chick," he replied.

"I'm just frustrated," I said. Of all the people to open up to... An old hippy couple at the top of a mountain! "We have one last red chair to get. One more! And it's way over on the last ridge. We can't afford to hire someone to take us there."

"Just like the government, man," said Forest. "Gotta crush the little dude."

"Something like that," I said before adding a "dude."

"You know, young wilderness man, life is like a journey," said Chick. "It's not about the destination. It's all the journey. And our journey should be love."

I didn't know what she was saying. Isn't life a journey *to* a destination?

"There's a saying I really dig," interrupted Forest. "There is freedom waiting for you in the breezes of the sky, and you ask, 'What if I fall?' Oh, but my darling, 'What if you fly?'"

"You mean I can fly to those red chairs?" I asked.

"You can do whatever your heart sets itself on," said Chick, showing her yellow teeth, or what was left of them, as she smiled.

"Uh, I need to go find my parents," I said.

"Look, son," said Forest. "Chill. I've been high up here many times, er, and I know how to fly to the fourth peak. Everyone goes on the top ridge or to the left of it. Nah. Dip a little below the ridge. On the right side. Just like, bypass the other summits. They'll distract you, man. Oh, and there's one psychedelic section. It's bad, dude. You got a ladder to success, though! Then you're like there. Copacetic?"

"I don't take things from strangers," I said.

"No, little dude!" laughed Forest. "Like, sound good?"

"Yeah, I think so."

"Then go fly!" said Chick. "Fly, little white dove, fly!"

"Maybe I will," I said, gathering my strength. "Maybe I will!"

I walked back to the interpretive center. How was I supposed to explain this to my parents? I decided to try something unusual. Something risky. Something unexpected. I was going to tell them the truth.

"Mom! Dad!" I shouted when I saw them standing inside the building. "I just met some old hippies! They said to go a little down from the ridge and to the right. Ignore the other summits, they said. And not to wonder about falling, but flying..." This was not panning out so well. "Like, flying like a white dove. Up high. We, er, can do it if it's a journey of love, er, and not a destiny. Our ladder of success..."

"Joey, are you okay?" asked Mom, concerned. I couldn't answer.

"I think he's trying to say that there is a better way to get to the fourth peak if we go to the right and a little down from the ridge and bypass the other peaks. Right?" said Dad.

"Copa...stetic? Copacetic?" I said.

Dad looked at Mom. She nodded. I smiled.

"Let's at least check it out," said Dad. "We'll go slow and safe. No falling."

"Only flying, dude," I said.

Also by the author, the Disconnected series:

ABOUT THE AUTHOR

D aniel J. Millette is a husband, father, writer, and
educator living in North East Saskatchewan. Millette has a love for meaningful storytelling, as well as for
mountain adventures with his family.

Please subscribe/like at YouTube, Facebook, Substack,
or all three.

🍁 ⚒ 🍁

"Go back?" he thought. "No good at all! Go sideways?
Impossible! Go forward? Only thing to do! On we
go!"
J.R.R. Tolkien, The Hobbit

www.ingramcontent.com/pod-product-compliance
Lightning Source LLC
LaVergne TN
LVHW041220080426
835508LV00011B/1013